# Roadscapes, a Sociopoetics of the Road

# Roadscapes, a Sociopoetics of the Road

Edited by

Catherine Morgan-Proux
and Leisha Ashdown-Lecointre

**Cambridge**
**Scholars**
Publishing

Roadscapes, a Sociopoetics of the Road

Edited by Catherine Morgan-Proux and Leisha Ashdown-Lecointre

This book first published 2023

Cambridge Scholars Publishing

Lady Stephenson Library, Newcastle upon Tyne, NE6 2PA, UK

British Library Cataloguing in Publication Data
A catalogue record for this book is available from the British Library

ISBN (10): 1-5275-3007-8
ISBN (13): 978-1-5275-3007-2

For Alan

It's the ancient road the soul knows
We always remember it when we see it
It beckons at birth
It carries us home

—from *Road* by Joy Harjo

# TABLE OF CONTENTS

# FOREWORD

## JEREMY BASSETTI

It is a cool June afternoon as I drive my white Toyota Camry rental across the Great Plains. Except for the sermons on AM radio, most of the stations are static out here. Though, the landscape—alien to me—is more than enough to hold my attention: prairie dogs pop up from their burrows and survey the area, bison munch on grass, a distant storm cell issues rain and probably hail, and the fragrance of wild sweetgrass and sage swirl into the car from a cracked window. Looming in the distance ahead of me is a silhouette of my destination: the Black Hills.

I have been on a road trip of sorts throughout the Black Hills doing research for a project. So, I couldn't decline when Catherine Morgan-Proux asked me to write the foreword for this new volume, *Roadscapes, a Sociopoetics of the Road*.

The road commands a special place in our collective imagination. On the one hand, the road stands for freedom, escape, and new beginnings. That feeling of freedom was not lost on me when I, a 16-year-old boy with a new driver's license, set off on the back roads of Central Florida in the mid-1990s to smoke cigarettes in the orange groves and far away from the prying eyes of my parents. As a young man, my dreams were colored by the great books, films, and songs of the road: *On the Road*, *Easy Rider*, and "Truckin'."

So mythic is the road in our collective imagination that we seldom envision the traffic jams, the interstate overpasses, the flat tires, the backaches, the high gasoline prices, our carbon emissions, and the billboards advertising fast food restaurants at each exit. We have sanitized these inconveniences from our imaginations, and what we envision is that liminal space through which one travels to not just encounter and learn about the world in its rawest form, but to find and learn a little bit about ourselves as we travel through it.

On the other hand, the road represents uncertainty and loneliness. As I sat alone at a bar one night in Custer, South Dakota, a young man pulled up a chair next to me. Over beers and bar food, Griffin told me he was on a road trip of his own. From Cincinnati he went north into Canada until the cold temperatures forced him to retreat south into the Dakotas, where I met him. His plan was to continue to Denver and "wherever the wind takes me." I asked him why he was on the road. "To figure things out. To clear my head," he said, his tone melancholy. I didn't pry. I didn't need to. I knew exactly what he was talking about.

As contradictory as it may seem, I've always found loneliness, especially when on the road, to be the great antidote to introversion, silence, and inaction. Yet the road, especially when mixed with loneliness, can also be an antidote to ignorance, says Mark Twain. When I was growing up, our teachers called the internet the "information superhighway." If the road is a type of connective tissue, then surely it is the kind found in the brain.

If not the road than the "information superhighway" helped Catherine Morgan-Proux and I meet each other online, during the lockdowns, and as we traveled through literature. I say "we" because reading is never really as solitary an act as we think, and because she, I, and her students had been reading some of the same books. She had assigned my podcast—Travel Writing World—to her graduate students enrolled in a course on travel literature at the University of Clermont Auvergne. I was delighted to learn her students had been reading travel books from authors like William Least Heat-Moon, Jack Kerouac, and Gloria Steinem because it is always delightful to see a new generation derive meaning and value from older work.

But the new generation must confront the specters ignored by the older ones. We might think that carbon emissions and climate change threaten our collective understanding of the road and our ability to travel on it. But if my encounter with the young man in Custer can illustrate any point, it must be that the allure and promise of the road—and our ability to draw meaning from it—are here to stay, for now.

Jeremy Bassetti, Ph.D.
Custer, South Dakota
June 2022

# ACKNOWLEDGEMENTS

We are appreciative of the *CELIS* research centre of Université Clermont Auvergne for their support of our research.

We are grateful to Carol Highsmith, visual documentarian, for her photograph, "Abandoned cars, Route 66, Arizona" (2006) from the Carol Highsmith's America archives of the Prints and Photographs division of the Library of Congress which features on the book cover and evokes the many layers of meaning in the idea of roadscapes.

Thank you to Jeremy Bassetti, host of the award-winning "Travel Writing World" podcast, for his very eloquent and touching foreword.

*Merci du fond du cœur* to Lynette Thorstensen for her creativity and for sharing her beautiful poetry inspired by memorable road trips.

We are indebted to Fran Van Wyk de Vries

Special thanks to our families for their encouragement.

# INTRODUCTION

## CATHERINE MORGAN-PROUX

This volume pays tribute to a rich tradition of how we imagine the road, our relationship to it and what it means to us. Representing the road is embedded in our language, in our lyrics and our literature, revealing the way we move through the world. We can say that the road is a site, peopled by a constellation of travellers, drivers, passengers, long distance voyagers, toll keepers, inn keepers and keepers of our dreams. Sometimes we are joined by the road, sometimes it separates us. Our ancient Western stories draw upon a shared culture of the road and its implications for our lives. It is on the road to Thebes that Oedipus enters into a road traffic argument about who should have right of way and ends up killing his father, one of the foundational myths of our Western culture.[1] It is at a crossroads that the first bluesman sells his soul to the devil in a Faustian exchange for a guitar.[2] And it is on the modern American highway that Wyatt and Billy breathe new life into cowboy mythology in *Easy Rider* (1969)[3], the film that became an essential part of 20th century iconography.[4]

This volume includes selected papers presented at an international seminar, *Roadscapes: A Sociopoetics of the Road* that took place at Université Clermont Auvergne in March 2020 with the support of the CELIS research centre. Since that event, the world has undergone the unprecedented situation of a global pandemic with repeated lockdowns and travel restrictions, whether over land, sea or air. In light of this, exploring our relationship to the road, its material reality and its cultural representations, seems a zeitgeist theme as people throughout the world have experienced a prolonged period when travel was profoundly disrupted. As we navigate the aftermath of this disruption, we are still working out the many ways in

---

[1] Philippe Artières, *Des routes. Accrochage* (Paris: Pauvert, 2018), 127.
[2] Eric Gonzalez, "In and Along the Mississippi. The Motif of Music in Joel and Ethan Coen's *O Brother, Where Art Thou?* and Jim Jarmusch's *Mystery Train*," *Revue française d'études américaines*, vol. no. 98, no. 4, 2003, 99.
[3] Dennis Hopper, 1969. Easy Rider. United States: Columbia Pictures.
[4] Lee Hill, *Easy Rider* (London: British Film Institute, 1996), 8.

which our relationship to travel has changed. The road, once taken for granted, has become a focal point for reflection.

The contributors to this volume have taken the long view on artistic and cultural representations of the road in the anglophone world of the 20th and 21st centuries. The chapters are in dialogue with the abundant and varied wealth of literary and artistic expression about and from the road, starting with, of course, Jack Kerouac's defining road trip narrative, *On the Road* (1957) which stunningly revealed the poetry of the tarmac or, as Kerouac put it: "The purity of the road. The white line in the middle of the highway unrolled and hugged our left front tyres, glued to our groove."[5] Kerouac's Counterculture novel also, crucially, framed a vision of the road as a site of unlimited freedom and mobility.[6] If the road is a text, it is a palimpsest. For generations, layers of poetry and prose have established the idea of the road as a site of exploration of self and country. Walt Whitman celebrated the joy of the "open road," in his humanist ode to life, "Song of myself" (1855). In his classic novel, *The Grapes of Wrath* (1939) John Steinbeck coined the phrase of the "Mother Road," for Route 66, conjuring up a promise of possibility to depression-era migrants. His 1962 road trip narrative *Travels with Charley* relates his trip "to try to rediscover this monster land."[7] His specially outfitted campervan is named Rocinante, after Don Quixote's horse, drawing on the quest tradition that has often underpinned travel literature. William Least Heat-Moon's *Blue Highways A Journey into America* (1982)[8] is a modern masterpiece in getting off the beaten track to explore the vanishing small towns of America and his own dwindling sense of self. This volume re-examines the foundational myths, motifs and markers of self-discovery in texts which represent the dynamics of the highway, while extending this literary focus to other artistic genres and perspectives. It is a timely publication in the Anthropocene era when it has become imperative to rethink our deep, complex relationship to roads and cars in order to imagine a sustainable future on a planet that can no longer afford to be powered by fossil fuel.

Understanding how our collective imaginary of the road informs and is informed by texts, both literary and artistic, requires an effective framework. Several important studies of road narratives have been published in recent

---

[5] Jack Kerouac, *On the Road* (London: Penguin Books, 2000), 121

[6] Ann Charters, Introduction to *On the Road* (London: Penguin Books, 2000), xxi.

[7] John Steinbeck, *Travels with Charley* (New York: Viking, 1962), 2

[8] William Least Heat-Moon, *Blue Highways. A Journey into America*, (New York: Back Bay Books, 1982)

years, most notably in the United States, and have usefully analyzed the genre in terms of its literary form, its function as a social critique and as a chronicle of American exploration of country and of self.[9] The critical lens of this volume is the sociopoetic approach. Developed by the French theorist, Alain Montandon of the *Centre de Recherche des Littératures et la Sociopoétique,* it is a lens that aims to enrich our understanding of the dialectical relationship between literature and society, an articulation between narrative and social interaction. According to Montandon's perspective, literature is both a reflection and a driving force of social dynamics:

> We consider sociopoetics less as a method than as a field of analysis which, fuelled by a culture of social representations as a pre-text, makes it possible to grasp the extent to which this pre-text participates in literary creation and poetics. It is less a question of sociocriticism, always more or less a victim of a conception of reflection, than of poetics in the etymological sense of the term, which considers social representations as dynamic elements of literary creation.[10]

In keeping with the sociopoetics stance, this volume adopts a wide, pluridisciplinary angle, including visual arts such as painting, cinema, and documentary film. As well as focussing on road texts, our volume asks questions about various aesthetics of the road. This is particularly pertinent considering the explicit project declared in our title *Roadscapes* to enquire about the pictorial value of the road. It refers to the road as a scene, the theatre of an unfolding journey, but also as scenery, the view shaped by human impulse to connect with our environment. Put another way, it is a consideration of landscape as artifact, an important mode of human signification, It echoes what Cosgrove, Daniels and Baker have phrased as, "a cultural image, a pictorial way of representing or symbolising

---

[9] Ronald Primeau, in *Romance of the Road* (1996), identifies four major tropes of American road narratives: "protest, the search for a national identity, self-discovery, and experimentation or parody" (15). Kris Lackey, in *RoadFrames: The American Highway Narrative* (1997) sees road narratives as the pervasive expression of American desire for freedom and national identity. Rowland A. Sherrill's *Road-Book America: Contemporary Culture and the New Picaresque* (2000) considers the road narrative as part of a picaresque literary tradition.

[10] Alain Montandon, "Sociopoétique" in Sociopoétiques [On line], 1 | 2016, posted 25 September 2020, consulted 14 July 2022. URL: http://revues-msh.uca.fr/sociopoetiques/index.php?id=640 (my translation)

surroundings."[11] The suffix "-scape" evokes not only the material substance of the road but, importantly for us, the way the human eye arranges and interprets its layers of meaning, whether what it sees is spectacular and salient or ordinary and invisible.[12]

In his contribution to the volume, Alain Montandon examines the pictorial representation of the American highway, stating from the outset that, despite the diversity of representations, it is part of a socio-cultural landscape of Americanness and produces a semiotic network with which to explore a sociopoetics of the road. His analysis of Crawford's artwork demonstrates that the road has become an industrial space, void of human presence, provoking a feeling of repeated alienation in the face of a very modern form of solitude. Drawing on the creative possibilities of different graphic art forms such as painting, collage, photography, pop art or conceptual art, American artists of the mid-twentieth century play with the framing of a whole or voluntarily truncated road. The artwork of Allan D'Arcangelo accentuates, for example, the saturation caused by a plethora of competing signs which, according to a Barthian terminology, represent a signifier detached from what it signifies. This reading is based on the pictorial *mise en abyme* of the windshield, described as a "screen" that transforms everyday observation into aesthetic vision.

Philippe Antoine also draws upon a visual medium in his chapter devoted to the documentary film, "Route One / USA" by Robert Kramer, shot during a six-month road trip taken by the film director and his crew along this East coast highway in 1987 to 1988. He points out how Kramer plays with the conventions of the road trip genre, favouring invention over adventure. The effect is a blurring of the lines between fiction and documentary to offer a historical, geographical, sociological and political portrait of the East Coast of small towns and rural landscapes drained after years of Reaganomics. The Route One road is a beaten track, which the camera regularly leaves to film conversations with people who inhabit the hinterland of roadscapes, territories that are not always visible from the highway. Indeed, the view is

---

[11] Denis Cosgrove, Stephen Daniels, Alan R. H. Baker, *The Iconography of Landscape: Essays on the Symbolic Representation, Design and Use of Past Environments* (Cambridge: Cambridge University Press, 1988), 1.

[12] "An ordinary road is just part of the invisible landscape of the everyday. [...] These everyday roads have penetrated our imaginations obliquely, not through myth and folklore of the great driving roads but through the compulsive habits and accidental poetry of the commonplace – or a reflex moan about the M4 bus lane." Joe Moran, *On Roads. A Hidden History.* (London: Profile Books, 2010), 2.

difficult to decipher in this film, and we are left with the impression of a fragmented, melancholy truth. Here, the road goes beyond its primary function of transit from frontier to frontier and is imbued with meaning that has everything to do with the construction and the unravelling of regional and national identity. The road, it seems, has the capacity to serve as a theatre where personal vulnerabilities and public voices intermingle, giving rise to the dynamic tensions that exist between them.

Fragmentary vision is also a finding of Lambert Barthélémy's study of movies and photographs, both American and European, inspired by the road. According to his reading, which is grounded in comparative literature analysis, the imaginary of displacement is of a hybrid nature and is made up of pieces of different possible orders resonating separately. Displacement reveals landscape, stimulates visual perceptions, and intensifies exploration of the visible. The films under study propose a version of the road as a space-in-itself. Their emphasis on detour, transit and immersion, and their questioning of the very notion of limit would suggest a re-invention of space itself. Lambert Barthélémy re-invests the term "roadwork" with a deconstructed rendering of space which encourages the audience to modify its perceptual frameworks from within, to see and feel differently. The "roadwork" of contemporary art defies the conventional function of the road as a place of consumer power and begs the question of its purpose when the road itself has become deculturalized. This process gives us insight into the road's hypnotic capture of reality, our gaze detached from a single imperative and drifting in postmodern subjectivity. A major finding of this study of film and photographs is that not only is there a road-space, but also a road-time, a movement of the dilation of the present in all its plurality. And even when the road is straight, it is certainly not straightforward. Transcontinental representations of the road, with its multiple turnings and interruptions, can be said to be a roadwork in progress.

This volume explores the meanings that we attach to roads in our collective imagination, the milestones that measure them, the borders they cross and the layers of stories they trace. Can we read roads as community versus individual spaces? Roads are, after all, classified by the highway code as either private or public. How do tourism routes and trails, for example, connect us to our shared heritage, both tangible and intangible? An interesting angle is to consider locales and regions in dynamic relation to the national roads that lead into and out of them.[13] Ted T. Cable provides us

---

[13] Andrew Edward Daigle, *Defining Highways: Regionalism, Routes and Circuits in American Road Literature* (Ph.D. diss., University of Colorado, 2016), 1.

with an insightful approach to re-visioning roadscapes that have too easily been dismissed as empty of meaning by professionals and the public alike. His chapter convincingly questions the hierarchy of values by which we judge the worthiness and the beauty of what we see from the road. It is based on research he carried out for his three published guidebooks to the Interstate 70 which crosses the states of Kansas, Missouri and Illinois, where agricultural landscapes have reputations for being monotonous and spaces to be endured, rather than enjoyed. For his analysis, Cable draws upon his expertise on the principles and applications of interpretation as laid out initially in Freeman Tilden's *Interpreting our Heritage* (1957).[14] Those principles have been shown to transform the travel experience from "empty" to engaging, entertaining and educational. Cable's study compellingly demonstrates how embracing those principles can transform the road travel experience from being "empty" to becoming engaging, entertaining, and educational.

Melanie Schneider considers the implications of the road as a collective experience in her analysis of the 2022 novel *Route One* by the French author Michel Moutot. In this fictional work, the construction in the late 1800s and early 1900s of the eponymous road along the Pacific coast is explored as a complex infrastructure project. Her chapter highlights how the novel delves into the concept of infrastructure as a vital network for society and explores the complex sociohistorical circumstances surrounding the birth of a major highway. As she points out, the novel highlights the imaginary of the American road and its role in shaping cultural perceptions and aspirations. Focussing on the concept of infrastructure, Schneider reveals the road as poetic space where public works meet private dreams.

In Isabel Oliveira's study of John Steinbeck's road narrative *Travels with Charley: In Search of America* published in 1962, we recognize the road as a route to self-recognition. Here the travelling writer takes to the road to rediscover and reconnect with a changing America. Significantly, as Oliviera emphasizes, Steinbeck's return to his hometown of Salinas, California, brings some soul-searching as he realizes the full extent of the changes that have occurred while he has remained disconnected. This reading of the text captures Steinbeck's attempt to reconcile his memories and experiences with the changing reality of his country.

---

[14] Freeman Tilden, *Interpreting our Heritage* (Chapel Hill: The University of North Carolina Press, 1957).

If the road trip is a "quintessential expression of Americanness"[15] what about other geographies and cultural identities for which roads carry meaning? Leisha Ashdown-Lecointre takes us to Ireland and offers us a reading of *Grace*, a novel by Paul Lynch where the road is represented as a site of human suffering and vulnerability. The novel reminds us of the historical reality of forced migration and in the case of Grace, the indignities of exile. The road here is a constant but also unchosen companion. It serves as a sort of escape route, providing an opportunity to survive through begging as well as stealing, as well as a symbol of a country's disintegration through recourse to forced labour. Unlike the American road with its inherent beauty as portrayed in many of the artistic works described in this volume, Paul Lynch comments that the road in his novel reflects the country's inability to build a sound infrastructure. Furthermore, Grace's plight is thrown into sharp relief due to her gender, as the narrative exposes her to the persistent menace and reality of sexual aggression. In a harsh, hostile earth, the road is both a place of danger for women but also a place to cling to in order to survive. Yet, in this *bildungsroman*, Grace does more than survive. Following the road takes her on a rite of passage from childhood to adulthood, via layers of her personal past and national memory. Interestingly, ghosts weave their way through the narrative and exert a prevailing impact on the eponymous heroine who attains a kind of state of *grace* herself, or in any case, an experience of the transcending power of the sacred.

This volume asks questions about intersections of genre and gender. The novel *Grace* begs the question, how do women's perceptions and experiences of the road reframe this traditionally masculine site of mobility? If the novel reminds us of the dangers of being on the road for women because of coerced displacement, what about women's agency on the road? What does a feminist road trip look like? In her collection of poetry, *Drive* (1998), Beat Generation artist, Hettie Jones offers a powerful portrait of herself as both "woman enough to be moved to tears / and man enough / to drive my car in any direction."[16] The activist Gloria Steinem's memoir *My*

---

[15] Anne Brigham, *American Road Narratives: Reimagining Mobility in Literature and Film* (Charlottesville: University of Virginia Press, 2015), 15.

[16] Hettie Jones, *Drive. Poems.* (Brooklyn, New York: Hanging Loose Press, 1998), 11. An anthology of women Beat poets edited by Annalisa Mari Pegrum and Sebastien Gavignet, *Beat Attitude; Femmes poètes de la Beat Generation* (Paris: Bruno Doucy, 2018) has recently been published in France and has shone a light on the women writers such as Hettie Jones, Diane di Prima, Lenore Kandel who have been long overlooked.

*Life on the Road* (2015) exalts the emancipatory energy of women on the move and urges her readers to embrace an "on-the-road state of mind."[17] Cultural representations of the road by women are remodelling our expectations for this genre.[18] Lynette Thorstensen's two poems, "Road Trip One" and "Road Trip Two," especially written for this volume, paint a roadscape in the colours of female friendship and sibling love. The two journeys described in the poems play with time, one tripping into the other through the memory of grief, both personal and collective. Whether it be the interrupted life of their travelling "sister" in "Road Trip One" or the mass removal of the aboriginal community, "the traditional owners" of the desert alluded to in "Road Trip Two," these poems are brave enough to face a sense of loss. The effect is both sorrowful and celebratory, offering us a vision of what a feminist road trip can look like. The itineraries of these two different road trips transcend geographical borders, "from Paris to Portugal," and, years later in the Australian desert, while transgressing societal borders of how women are conventionally meant to dress or behave. Sharing the wheel and a wildness of heart, the women in these poems are inventing their own highway code.

Re-invention is at the centre of *I the Road* by the "writer of a writer," Ross Goodwin, and published by JBE Books represented in this volume by its editor, David Desrimais. As he outlines in the interview here, David

---

[17] "My [...] purpose is to encourage you to spend some time on the road, too. By that, I mean traveling – or even living for a few days where you are – in an on-the-road state of mind, not seeking out the familiar but staying open to whatever comes along. It can begin the moment you leave your door. Like a jazz musician improvising, or a surfer looking for a wave, or a bird riding a current of air, you'll be rewarded by moments when everything comes together." Gloria Steinem, *My Life on the Road* (New York: Random House, 2015), xxi.

[18] Elinor Nauen's anthology *Ladies, Start your Engines. Women Writers on Cars and the Road*, (Winchester, MA: Faber and Faber, 1996) stands out as a particularly rich collection of road texts authored by women. More recently, Mariella Frostrup has edited an anthology, *Wild Women and their Amazing Adventures over Land, Sea and Air* (London: Head of Zeus, 2019) which includes texts by women at the car wheel or on motorbikes such as Edith Wharton, Ella Maillart and Lois Pryce. An important, growing body of researchers have analysed women's road narratives using feminist, cultural and literary theory that has completely opened up this traditionally male genre, for example Alexander Ganser, *Roads of Her Own: Gendered Space and Mobility in American Women's Road Narratives*, 1970-2000. (New York: Rodopi, 2009) and Jessica Envold's Ph.D. dissertation, *Women on the Road : Regendering Narratives of Mobility*, Göteborgs Universitet/Karlskrona Tekniska Högskola, (2003).

Desrimais was motivated to publish this text because of its fascinating re-invention of Kerouac's iconic road trip narrative. The ingenuity of Goodwin's approach is to harness the creativity of Artificial Intelligence through which he transforms a car into a kind of giant, mobile typing machine. Following in the tracks of Kerouac's *On the Road*, after having absorbed the literary roadscapes (and railscapes) of hundreds of texts fed into the machine, all the while reacting to actual roadscapes through a camera, it is a unique experiment in roadscape re-creation. We are tempted to call this process, a road*scope*. The suffix "scope" acknowledges the incorporation of an instrument – and digital technology - in the viewing / writing process and the unpredictable, immeasurable, borderless text that it generates. Rooted in the very recent research in Artificial Neural Network, *1 the Road*, invites a thoroughly novel reflection on the articulation and authority of the author in the era of machines. Who, exactly, is at the wheel?

How thrilling it is to conclude this volume with a chapter that defies conventional notions of closure and instead serves as a gateway to explore new horizons in the representation of roadscapes, thereby enhancing our comprehension of sociopoetics. This final chapter offers an invigorating exploration that opens up fresh perspectives, allowing us to delve deeper into the intricate network of roadscapes and broaden our understanding of the dynamic interplay between society and creativity. Between *On the Road* and *1 the Road (*or *One the Road,* we might say)*,* there is merely a letter "e" that is different. Perhaps this "e" stands for exploration, that fundamental sense of curiosity for new ways of seeing that all the studies in this volume share.

# Bibliography

Artières, Philippe. *Des routes. Accrochage.* Paris: Pauvert, 2018.

Barthes, Roland. *Elements of Semiology.* New York: Hill and Wang, 1973.

Brigham, Anne. *American Road Narratives: Reimagining Mobility in Literature and Film,* Charlottesville: University of Virginia Press, 2015.

Cosgrove, Denis, Stephen Daniels, and Alan R. H. Baker. *The Iconography of Landscape: Essays on the Symbolic Representation, Design and Use of Past Environments,* Cambridge: Cambridge University Press, 1988

Daigle, Andrew Edward. *Defining Highways: Regionalism, Routes and Circuits in American Road Literature* Ph.D. diss., University of Colorado, 2016.

Envold, Jessica. "Women on the road : Regendering Narratives of Mobility," Ph.D. diss. Göteborgs Universitet/Karlskrona Tekniska Högskola, 2003

Frostrup, Mariella. Ed. *Wild Women and their Amazing Adventures over Land, Sea and Air*. London: Head of Zeus, 2019.

Ganser, Alexandra. "On the Asphalt Frontier: American Women's Road Narratives, Spatiality, and Transgression." *Journal of International Women's Studies*, 7(4), (2006). 153-167.

—. *Roads of Her Own: Gendered Space and Mobility in American Women's Road Narratives*, 1970-2000. New York: Rodopi, 2009

Gonzales, Eric. "In and Along the Mississippi. The Motif of Music in Joel and Ethan Coen's O Brother, Where Art Thou? and Jim Jarmusch's Mystery Train," *Revue française d'études américaines*, vol. no 98, no. 4, 2003, 99-110.

Heat-Moon, William Least. *Blue Highways. A Journey into America*. New York: Back Bay Books, 1982.

Hill, Lee. *Easy Rider*. London: British Film Institute, 1996.

Hopper, Dennis. *Easy Rider*. United States: Columbia Pictures, 1969.

Jones, Hettie. *Drive*. Brooklyn, New York: Hanging Loose Press, 1998.

Kerouac, Jack. *On the Road*. London: Penguin Books, 2000.

Lackey, Kris. *Roadframes. The American Highway Narrative*. Lincoln: University of Nebraska Press, 1997.

Montandon, Alain. "Sociopoétique" in *Sociopoétiques* [online], 1 | 2016, posted 25 September 2020, consulted 14 July 2022. URL : http://revues-msh.uca.fr/sociopoetiques/index.php?id=640

Moran, Joe. *On Roads. A Hidden History*. London: Profile Books, 2010.

Nauen, Elinor. Ed. *Ladies, Start your Engines. Women Writers on Cars and the Road*. Winchester, MA: Faber and Faber, 1996.

Pegrum, Annalisa Mari, and Sebastien Gavignet. *Beat Generation. Femmes poètes de la Beat Generation*. Paris: Editions Bruno Doucy, 2018.

Primeau, Ronald. *Romance of the Road. The Literature of the American Highway*. Bowling Green: Popular Press, 1996.

Sherrill, Rowland A. *Road-Book America: Contemporary Culture and the New Picaresque*. Champaign: University of Illinois Press, 2000

Steinem, Gloria. *My Life on the Road*. New York: Random House, 2015.

Steinbeck, John. *The Grapes of Wrath*. Harlow: Penguin Books, 2017.

—. *Travels with Charley; in Search of America*. New York: Viking Press, 1962.

Tilden, Freeman. *Interpreting our Heritage*. Chapel Hill: The University of North Carolina Press, 1957.

Whitman, Walt. *Leaves of Grass*. Penguin Clothbound Poetry. London: Penguin Classics, 2017.

# CHAPTER ONE

# PICTORIAL EXPRESSIONS OF THE GREAT AMERICAN HIGHWAYS, WITH PARTICULAR REFERENCE TO RALSTON CRAWFORD AND ALLAN D'ARCANGELO

## ALAIN MONTANDON

There are many representations of the road but there are also fundamentals which are well established in American culture by the end of the 20th century, despite the diversity of social cultures. This diversity is, of course, displayed in the different forms of representations, both literary and pictorial, as well as in the different temperaments of the artists. We will see, for example, that for Edward Hopper the road is merely there. It is not a road of communication. It is, rather, deserted, and void of signs (it is the garage which bears the signs). In short, the road seems mute. On the contrary, for D'Arcangelo the road is entirely made up of signs. Yet profound connections, intentional or not, do exist between the artists. Despite their different styles and mental images, one finds similar understandings of the American road.

Let us begin with a reminder that a sociopoetics of the road starts with looking at social representations and the socio-cultural imaginary, observing how they inform literary and artistic creations. In the specific case of the American road, it can be noted that there are different representations of it, but that, through this diversity, there are essential features in American culture that come partly from history and partly from the physical conditions of the geography and layout of American roads. Obviously, Route 66 has famously become a mythical space in America, a transcontinental road that is part of the national cultural landscape, time and time again represented, described, photographed, whether in literature "the mother road, the road of flight" of John Steinbeck in *The Grapes of Wrath[1]*, in films such as *Easy Rider[2]*, or in songs.

As Caroline Croubières puts it, "the 'semiotic complex' of Route 66 asserts its visual identity, through a whole stock of signifiers that shape its imaginary."[3] Firstly, there is an 'American-ness', a commonly shared, widespread notion, even though the stereotype is difficult to define. What appears in the image of the American road is, on the one hand, a movement of displacement, a dynamism of passage, of a long transition due to the tremendous distances of the American territory and its accompanying monotony and solitude, such as the cinema has staged. On the other hand, the landscape is revealed or destroyed by displacement, and becomes a dilated, serial, and repetitive space.

This repetition is found in Ed Ruscha's work through the succession of twenty-six photographs of gasoline stations that make up the artist's book *Twentysix Gasoline Stations,[4]* produced by him in 1963: "A series of photographs following each other in a more or less equal rhythm."[5] Route 66 has its own sense of movement, while imposing its rhythm on those who use it. Route 66 constructs its identity as a space characterised by its direction and as a "typically American" place.

The artist Ed Ruscha was born in 1937 in Omaha, Nebraska, and lives now in California. He belongs to the pop and conceptual art movement, alongside artists such as Roy Lichtenstein, Jasper Johns and Andy Warhol. In 1961, Dennis Hopper, who directed and starred in *Easy Rider* (1969) a few years later, took a photo of a petrol station that probably inspired Ed Ruscha. The notion of "Double Standard" is humorous because standard is a banal term, designating a mark of uniformity, but it is also the name of an oil company, the Standard Oil Company. Dennis Hopper met Duchamp in Pasadena in 1963 and was won over by his artistic ideas: "Duchamp said that the artist of the future would not be a painter but an individual who

---

[1] Paris, Gallimard, 1947, chap. XII, 164

[2] Dennis Hopper, 1969. *Easy Rider*. United States: Columbia Pictures.

[3] Caroline Courbières, "Dans le sillage du mythe : rémanence de la route 66," *Communication & langages*, PUF, mars 2018, n°195, 59-76, p. 66. "le "complexe sémiotique" de la Route 66 va affirmer son identité visuelle, par tout un stock de signifiants qui facetteront son imaginaire."

[4] See Art Gallery of New South Wales, https://www.artgallery.nsw.gov.au/collection/works/427.2008.a-vv.

[5] Ed Ruscha, *Huit textes Vingt-trois entretiens : 1965-2009*, Zürich, JRP Ringier, 2010, 164.

would point to something and declare it to be art. That's what the finger meant to me. That's what the photographer does with his camera."[6] Ed Ruscha's composition does not aim to reproduce the real, but to explore the idea of representation: "it is not a real representation, but a combination of many things."[7]

His book *Twentysix Gasoline Stations* is the result of a series of small, sober photographs in a seemingly random arrangement, underlining the fact that any classification or hierarchy is impossible and that the number of photos could be indefinite. Such a photographic inventory speaks volumes about this "serialization" which appears to be a trait of "American-ness" (already revealed by Kafka in "Amerika" or "The Man who Disappeared"). This book was refused by the Library of Congress because of its non-conformism.

Ed Ruscha also uses his photographs in the form of paintings through which he reworks the graphic aspect of the gas station as object. With the series of "*Standard Stations*" (*Standard Station, Amarillo, Texas* (1963), *Standard Station* (1966), *Burning Gas Station* (1966), *Burning Standard* (1968), *Standard Station* (1986-1987), Ed Ruscha draws upon Pop Art and Conceptual Minimalism to produce a variation on the same theme. He is fascinated by its familiarity yet slight otherness. Some, like the painting of a burning petrol station, reveal an underlying fantasy. One can certainly see in it a dangerous *auto-da-fé* of capitalism. We suggest that, much less than a political stance, it is rather the self-destruction of painting itself which becomes an obsessional theme, one that is imposed by society. This self-annihilation foreshadows a trend that would become very public with the *Girl with Balloon* painting by Banksy destroyed on 8th October 2018 at Sotheby's auction in London.

It is important to stress how much photographic art conceived by these artists has influenced their work: "The photograph showed me what the object looked like when it was laid flat. From then on, I didn't have to make the adjustments from life. Other artists transpose the three dimensions of the real world into a two-dimensional image. Photography did that for me."[8]

---

[6] Isabelle Regnier, 2008. "Denis Hopper : "Je brisais constamment les règles."" *Le Monde* 22/10/2008 https://www.lemonde.fr/cinema/article/2008/10/21/dennis-hopper-je-brisais-constamment-les-regles_1109377_3476.html.

[7] *Ibid.*

[8] Quoted in https://blog.artsper.com/fr/la-minute-arty/ed-ruscha-echographie-de-lamerique/

Seeing things photographically predisposes one to apprehend reality in the same way as a motorist driving on a motorway, that of "looking at flat landscapes."[9]

With other artists, matter changes without fundamentally altering. Consider a famous painter like Edward Hopper, who is said to express an authentic 'Americanness.' Roads feature rarely in his paintings perhaps because of his preference for the subway and the train[10]. However, there is one particularly interesting painting, *Gas station*, from 1940. Some critics have stated that it looks like a photo, but this is not so. In fact, the painter worked with several photographs of a gas station near Truro. The reason we mention this is that there is a very close relationship between painting and photography in the representation of the road and many painters are also photographers.

Let us return to Hopper's painting. The gas station stands as a port, a landmark in the dimness of the road at night. It is like a threshold, facing the unlimited immensity of a dark, murky, unfathomable, alienating, threatening, even mortifying road. The gas station attendant is a sort of Cerberus, guarding the passage to the realm of the dead or the underworld. He has a mythological stature, and it is true that "Hopper often paints the profound banality of a suburban landscape with the care devoted to a sacred scene.[11]" The accentuated perspective converges on the end of the road, the dark point where it will disappear, and the gas station is the last outpost before the lifeless road. The light, both natural and artificial, gives the liminal space of the petrol station and its attendant at dusk an underlying sense of drama, reinforced by the tongues of light emitted from the right, and the tree branch that passes the billboard, with its ominous tentacles. It is also noticeable that the dry, russet-coloured grass runs parallel to the road like lines of fire, as if the red of the petrol pumps had given them direction and speed, a flamboyant dynamism, suggesting the road is an infernal fire. The pump attendant, alone and in a bent-over position, seems to be engaged in an occupation that is unclear. Is he cleaning, checking, adjusting the pumps? It certainly keeps him there in a ritual that could be interpreted as a

---

[9] *Ibid.*

[10] "I've always liked approaching a big city by train [...] you feel a bit of fear and anxiety, but at the same time you have a great visual interest in the things you see." See Alain Montandon, "Nuits intimes et inimitiés nocturnes" in *Staging American Nights*, revue *Miranda*, 20, 2020, http://journals.openedition.org/miranda/24239.

[11] Alain Cueff, *Edward Hopper. Entractes*, (Paris : Flammarion 2012), 151.

kind of worship, for these three pumps resemble idols from a modern mythology represented by Pegasus, the winged horse of the *Mobil* oil brand.

The familiar scene is propelled into an archaic past, and one critic has interpreted the scene as a trap in which it is no longer the cars that feed off the pumps, but the pumps that feed off the cars in an inversed reality. The absence of cars and the gas station attendant's outfit, which makes him "a priest in civilian dress" both reinforce this reading. There is a cannibalistic or vampiric aspect that also contributes to such an ambivalent, frightening vision offered of the road and the anxiety it arouses. The liminal situation is underlined by oppositions: between natural light and artificial light, between the disappearing, natural world, and the extension of the modern industrial world represented by the gas station serving the symbol of the "American way of life" represented by the car. The gaze that the gas station attendant turns towards this representation of modernity, far from expressing a form of liberation, bears witness to a kind of alienation. Here the road, paradoxically, refers to a fundamental absence of communication, leaving the attendant, symbolic of humankind, doomed to solitude.

We see this illustrated in another canvas by Hopper. *Four Lane Road*, from 1956, depicts the same gas station attendant, still well dressed, sitting outside a house, staring absently, it would seem, at the setting sun on a four-lane road, with two lanes separated by a central median. Here the absence of communication is signified by the multiplication of opposing components in a mortifying process of doubling. It begins with the dark shadow of the seated figure, the first doubling, followed by the pairing of the two pumps, one on the man's side and the other through the window, on the woman's side. She is berating the man, perhaps because of his passivity, while she, full of energy, seems reproachful of his nostalgia for nature, for light and stillness, and longing for a freedom from the alienating effects of modern work. The woman is all the more castrating because the idea of a possible decapitation is represented, with a touch of humour, by the window blind. The tragic alienation is visible in the parallel between the man's head and that of the pump, which is paired with the second head in the form of the shadow in symmetry with the second pump. This opposition of forces is found in the contrast of yellow and red that structures the canvas.

This mysterious, deadly world generated by communication channels that lead nowhere is also the subject of the paintings of Ralston Crawford (1906-1978), who was both a painter and a photographer. Ralston Crawford is known for his abstract representations of urban and industrial life, which led him to a geometrization of the landscape. *Overseas Highway* (1940) highlights the vanishing point of a perspective that reveals both the emptiness of a vehicle-free road and, with the serialization of the pavement plates, the indefiniteness of a road that seems to lead nowhere. The absence of human presence turns the road into a cold, mineral place. It comes as no surprise to learn that another painting from 1941 is called *Gray Street*. Similarly, the painting *Whitestone Bridge* (1940) further emphasises the unreal character of these constructions. Through these representations, we see that the motorway requires a kind of purification of lines and contents, producing an *Entfremdung* effect, or a strangeness, as if the motorway were experienced as a lifeless, wordless, deserted world.

The pop artist Alfred Leslie transforms the overwhelming banality of the road in his subtle pieces that play, as Thierry Dufrêne notes, on contrasting blacks and whites.[12] Above all, his work conveys a kind of ghostly image and a way of revealing the unearthly quality of subjects. Leslie took the risk of drawing while driving his car across the US from west to east on his way back from a 1977 trip from California to Amherst, Massachusetts. The images reworked in his studio resulted in a book, *100 Views Along the Road,* published in 1988. These black and white watercolours are inspired by the Japanese concept of *notan*, which implies the balance of white and black in art.[13]

The very title of *One Hundred Views Along the Road* clearly echoes the views of Mount Fuji and the Tokaido Road depicted by Hokusai and especially Hiroshige. *Drive-in Movie* (1978-81) by Leslie bears witness to the repetitive and serial character of the hundred views process. In this work, Dufrêne noted that there was a new, nocturnal internalization of the theme of the road. It is a question of rendering the feeling of the space of the road, and the emotion felt by the landscape glimpsed through the endless ribbon of the American road. While Leslie plays on the tradition of nineteenth-century travel, he transforms detail and light effects in a way that points to abstraction. Consider the photographic effect of a painting of 'light as painting' such as in Leslie's *Black and white watercolor*. The highway appears black, lined, and covered with white road signs and threatening clouds, like a pre-apocalyptic photograph. This view conveys a sense of vertigo, of loss, through the movement of the watercolour brushstrokes that

---

[12] Thierry Dufrêne, "On the Road again," Gallimard, *Les Cahiers de médiologie*, 1996/2, n° 2, 173-179.

[13] This Japanese aesthetic was disseminated in America by Arthur Wesley Dow whose 1899 publication *Composition* was reprinted multiple times until the end of the 20th century.

seem to presage a dissolution of the landscape and a feeling of fluctuating identity, threatened by mists. Finally, *Highway View* is exemplary of the inherent violence provided by the road signs that impose themselves on and violate the landscape with their artificial, flat and hard geometric forms, opposed to the gradations and nuances of the watercolour tones. These aggressive and arbitrary tones of white balance the dark masses according to the *notan* concept.

Later, Leslie turned to figurative painting, as shown in *Location Shooting* (1997-1990), where the road appears as a wound. The very title of this work, alluding to the world of cinema, reminds us that Kerouac was influenced by the film culture of his time, most notably by the panoramic western landscapes of John Ford. Leslie's route here is indeed a "shooting," the cameraman having replaced the photographer. Leslie himself made a film, *Pull my Daisy* (1959) adapted by Jack Kerouac from the third act of his *Beat Generation* play. The double yellow stripe reminds us that the road is above all a sign, not a language, but an ideogram,[14] or rather an assembly of ideograms contributing to its mythical dimension.

With Allan D'Arcangelo (1930- 1998), who focuses solely on the signs that line the highways, we move towards an even more pronounced abstraction. To approach the original body of this artist's work, let us begin by recalling the semiological system as set out by Roland Barthes in his *Mythologies* which distinguishes between signifier, sign and signified. This will help us understand the signposting interpretation of the road in terms of D'Arcangelo who mainly depicted roads and road signs. An abstract expressionist and pop artist, his paintings are reminiscent of Chirico as well as Dali in the way that the proliferation of signs turns into a form of surrealism and humour. He appropriates typically American advertising images, advertisements, and road signs, and at the same time, creates a distancing by proposing them as works of art.

In *June Moon 1963* (1969), he gives an almost cinematic image of the movement of a car, at night, driving towards a gas station whose orange sign, with the Gulf brand, progressively takes the place of the moon and dominates the scene. His paintings of the road underline our separation from the natural world. The 1963 painting *Moon* is exemplary in this respect, with the moon - or whatever represents it - being eroded by an indistinct dark mass. Added to this is the dramatic perspective of a white band that

---

[14] Roland Barthes, "Le Mythe aujourd'hui," *Mythologies* (Paris : Éditions du Seuil, 1957), 213.

disappears in the centre of the painting, in the black of the night. We say "dramatic" because this term was used by David d'Angers to characterise the romantic painting of Caspar David Friedrich, who spoke of the "dramatisation of the landscape." Robert Rosenblum has demonstrated the legacy of the German Romantic painters on contemporary painting[15] and this same pictorial dramatization can be found here, in his landscape of the moon. (Obviously, the underlying meaning is no longer the same, despite the presence of a certain nihilism and despair).

The subjective view in *The Holy Family* (1980) is interesting for its surreal humour. The rear-view mirror, from which baby shoes hang, reflects and duplicates the image of the road. The road ahead and behind is infinite (we know that parallel lines only meet at infinity). Do the baby shoes mean that childhood and walking are mere memories for an entirely motorised adult world? Here again, what is striking in these representations of the road is the cruel symmetry, the monotony and the solitude of a world deserted by the human figure. In many of the paintings, advertising signs are displayed, overlaid, just like the motorway signs in U.S. *Highway I, No. 4* (1962). To fill this despairing monotony and the absence of meaning, the painter adds erotic, fantasy images taken from a cigarette advertisement, as in *Smoke Dream 1* (1963) or in *Smoke Dream 2* (1963).

*Rainbow Highway pro 51* (1977) mixes different signs in a humorous way, suggesting that the apparent emptiness of the road is, as it turns out, saturated with information. This information has little meaning in the end. It exists only as a signifying sign without a signified, as shown by the incoherent double sign, its black lines echoing those of the road, or the small guiding lines on a green square background that seems to obstruct the road. All these motorway signs, like advertising posters according to Baudrillard, erase the landscape, supplant it. We could go as far as saying they cancel it out.[16]

In a similar register, *Morning Star (Texaco)* (1980) humorously expresses the incoherence of signs in the advertising world of petrol brands. So many signs to signal that roads are not straight (*Four Square* (1964)) and what we see from the car (*Minnesota Morning*, (1978)) with a *trompe l'œil* effect, are telegraph wires that block the road perspective. Paul Virilio notes that the

---

[15] Robert Rosenblum, *Modern Painting and the Northern Romantic Tradition. Friedrich to Rothko*. (London : Thames and Hudson, 1975).
[16] Jean Baudrillard, *Simulacres et simulation*, (Paris: Galilée, 1981), 138.

windscreen functions as a screen,[17] emphasising the fact that this individual mode of transport transforms our existential experience of the world into an aesthetic vision.

Let us finish our discussion of D'Arcangelo with a painting of a barrier blocking the road. *Landscape* is crossed by a horizontal strip that defensively breaks the momentum of perspective, the space of the canvas playing with flatness and depth. The series called "Barriers" and the series called "Constellation" (over 120 paintings) apply barriers to the road in perspective, highlighting protruding patterns crossing the canvas against a white background (*Bridge-Barrier* and *Barrier #3*). What has been called minimalism and precisionism in D'Arcangelo's work reveals the emptiness of a sign-saturated Americanness.

In conclusion, the road is no longer the mythical space of the new frontier, nor even the agonising crossroads of Hitchcock's *North by Northwest* (1959)[18] where anything can happen. It has become an abstract reality, revealing the end of adventure and human failure, reflecting the disillusionment and disenchantment of a representation of the American road in the consciousness of this generation, where abstract expressionism has given way to the invasion of signage. To quote Thierry Dufrêne, we could say that the road is a sign of the times.[19]

Translation: Catherine Morgan-Proux

# Bibliography

Barthes, Roland. "Le Mythe aujourd'hui," *Mythologies*, Paris, Éditions du Seuil, 1957.
Baudrillard, Jean. *Simulacres et simulation*, Paris, Galilée, 1981.
Courbières, Caroline. "Dans le sillage du mythe : rémanence de la route 66," *Communication & langages*, PUF, mars 2018, n°195, 59-76.
Cueff, Alain. *Edward Hopper. Entractes*, Flammarion 2012.

---

[17] P. Virilio, *Traverses*, n°10, "Le simulacre," Centre Georges Pompidou, 1978

[18] Ernest Lehman, Alfred Hitchcock, Cary Grant, Eva Marie Saint, James Mason, Jessie Royce Landis, Leo G. Carroll, Martin Landau, and Bernard Herrmann. 2000. *North by Northwest*. Burbank, CA: Warner Home Video.

[19] Translator note. In the original text the author quotes Thierry Dufrêne as saying "*la route est tombée dans le panneau*," which literally means "the road has fallen into the trap."

Dufrêne, Thierry. "On the Road again," Gallimard, *Les Cahiers de médiologie*, 1996/2, n° 2, 173-179.

Hopper, Dennis. 1969. *Easy Rider*. United States: Columbia Pictures, 95 min.

Montandon, Alain. "Nuits intimes et inimitiés nocturnes" in *Staging American Nights*, revue *Miranda*, 20, 2020.
http://journals.openedition.org/miranda/24239

Regnier, Isabelle. 2008. "Denis Hopper : "Je brisais constamment les règles."" *Le Monde* 22/10/2008
https://www.lemonde.fr/cinema/article/2008/10/21/dennis-hopper-je-brisais-constamment-les-regles_1109377_3476.html

Rosenblum, Robert. *Modern Painting and the Northern Romantic Tradition. Friedrich to Rothko*. Thames and Hudson, London, 1975.

Ruscha, Ed. *Huit textes Vingt-trois entretiens: 1965-2009*, Zürich: JRP Ringier, 2010.

Steinbeck, John. *The Grapes of Wrath*, translated into French as *Les Raisins de la Colère*, Paris, Gallimard, 1947, chap. XII, 164.

Virilio, P. *Traverses*, n°10, "Le simulacre," Centre Georges Pompidou, 1978.

# CHAPTER TWO

# A ROAD, A COUNTRY AND A PEOPLE. ON *ROUTE ONE / USA* BY ROBERT KRAMER

## PHILIPPE ANTOINE

For six months in 1987 and 1988, Robert Kramer and a small team followed US Route 1 running along the Atlantic coast of the USA for 5000 km, with the idea of making a film.[1] The work blurs the border between fiction and documentary, uses both a historical and geographical approach, proposes a political and sociological viewpoint on Reagan's America (on the eve of the elections which brought George Bush to power), and allows us to hear the most diverse opinions. This special "country portrait"[2], embedded in travelling time, helps us to question the configuration of a genre, the "road movie", from which it departs on several levels. *Route One / USA* is certainly a "film in motion"[3] but it does not exalt speed, freedom, the unknown or free nature. The road as such is not the real topic and the most important aspect is the stages and numerous encounters with communities and people inhabiting it. The shots featuring it are essentially breaths between the sequences Kramer retained and edited (4 hours from 70 hours of rushes)[4]. However, if the road isn't a setting, (and even less a backdrop),

---

[1] *Route One / USA*, Les Films d'Ici / La Sept Paris, 1989, 255 mins. The film is divided into two equal parts. References to the film are henceforth given in the body of the text (part number followed by the timing of the sequence).

[2] I'm borrowing this term from David Martens, "Qu'est-ce que le portrait de pays ? Esquisse de physionomie d'un genre mineur." (*Poétique*, Number 184, 2018/2), 247-268.

[3] Kramer affirms that he has to "confront the idea of a film in motion which isn't a road movie, which doesn't have the look of a reckless displacement through its setting" (Bernard Eisenschitz, *Points de départ. Entretien avec Robert Kramer*, (Aix-en-Provence, Institut de l'Image, 2001),118.

[4] In a recorded interview with Serge Daney (1989), Kramer gives some information about the making of his film. No prepared scenario had been written in advance and after five months of filming, during editing, this quasi documentary took shape. The

it is the "vehicle of meaning"[5] according to which a personal relationship with the territory is expressed. The great filmmaker confirmed in an interview, "I make films which are the experience I have of things and issues."[6] *Route One* is effectively the visualisation of a lived and perceived space, of a country shaken by successive crises shown by the documentarian in the course of the work and finally the story of more or less successful attempts to understand an often chaotic and illegible world.

## Doc, Robert and Kramer: one and three roads

Kramer belongs to a fairly rare category of American filmmakers exiled in Europe, and more particularly in France. His film is the story of a return, ten years later, to his native country.[7] One character, Doc,[8] played by Paul McIsaac, sets out to visit the country and meet the inhabitants and we follow him for nearly the entire film. He constantly plays the role of taking the pulse of human and social realities. Through him, encounters documenting a widely diverse itinerary take place: from the North to the South, on the East coast, from the birth of the USA to the state of the country at the beginning of the 90s, within different ethnic and social groups and according to a personal history indirectly informing certain film sequences. One example will suffice: at the Fort Bragg military base, Doc (the character) recalls a soldier's past which is also that of Paul (the man) by

---

interview is available at the following address: http://derives.tv/entretien-sonore-entre-robert-kramer-et-serge-daney/ [consulted on 14/03/22].

[5] Concerning the photographers of the Federal Security Agency, Anne Baldasari writes: "For them, the road becomes something more than a specific "setting"; it attains the status of a vector of meaning expressing in a cultural way the relationship to the territory that is specifically "American" ("La photographie, la route, le territoire. Introduction aux paysages véhiculaires." (*Cahiers de la photographie*, no. 14, *Le Territoire*, 1984), 18. This analysis could in my opinion easily be transposed to Kramer's film.

[6] This comment is extracted from Jeanine Euvrard, "Entretien avec Robert Kramer." (*24 Images*, no. 92, 1998), 34.

[7] The fact of having been absent for a long time allows us to understand better the country seen again and quite obviously to be more sensitive to the changes that have taken place.

[8] He is the only fictional character in the film - his presence is still enough to weaken the border between documentary and fiction which for Kramer shouldn't exist. See for example *Points de départ*, (*op. cit.*, 78). We note in passing that the doctor has been one of the mandatory figures of travel stories, at least since the nineteenth century. He is the one who, because of his profession and skills, is able to *diagnose* the ills suffered by a people and a country.

simulating a parachute jump in front of Robert [*Part Two*, 00: 53][9]. The spectator hears Doc's voice as well as those of his successive interlocutors. Yet there is another imposing presence, that of the tour operator filming the countryside as well as the meetings and dialogue with Doc or the other protagonists in the documentary. This example should not be confused with the author, director and signatory of the film, Robert Kramer, even if he is effectively behind the camera.

This rapid overview of the mechanism put in place in *Route One/USA*[10] helps us to take into account the cultural and social representations of Route 1. Kramer, Robert and Doc share the same basic values and judgments about the state of the country. Depending on the different types of presence in the film, the three of them show a real empathy with those for whom the American dream has turned into a nightmare. Having said that, this common vision, like the unequivocally critical perspective of the work, is powerfully conveyed by the diversity of levels on which it functions and by the distancing that results from this enunciative layering. The three roads portrayed in the film are both different and similar.

Doc lives in his own world. We see him diving into deep water early in the film, then reading the first stanza of *Song of the Open Road* (*Part One*, 00.03),[11] roaming in a forest devastated by logging, taking the pulse of the America of the end of the 80s, exploiting different means of locomotion, lingering in front of commemorative monuments, and adapting to different groups of people he meets with real ease by frequently participating in his hosts' activities. Quite logically, he inherits the task of *experiencing* the trip (and, besides, Paul McIsaac possesses considerable latitude for the filming

---

[9] "This simulation sequence takes on an undeniable importance for both the film status of the character and the staging of memory and History" Caroline Boué, "L'identité en marche dans *Route One/USA* de Robert Kramer." (*Tumultes*, no. 10, April 1998), 253.

[10] For a more precise analysis of this point, see Lise Gantheret, "L'énonciation personnelle du film." (*Cahiers Louis-Lumière*, no. 8, 2011), 100-118.

[11] Here are the verses by Walt Whitman: "Afoot and light-hearted I take to the open road, / Healthy, free, the world before me, / The long brown path before me leading wherever I choose." As Caroline Boué notes (*art. cit.*, 248), this America no longer exists and Doc knows that what awaits him does not correspond in any way with the poet's vision.

and selection of certain scenes).[12] Even if adventure undeniably predominates in *Route One*'s inventory, (unlike the "canonical" *road movie* plot that inherits elements from the picaresque novel), the spectator is encouraged to follow a character for whom nothing of importance really happens even if it is through his meeting people that any form of contact takes place. During a fine film sequence, he has a friendly discussion and drinks with a local inhabitant who has set up his home on the roadside in a vacant lot overhanging it [*Part One*, 0:46]. The scene has evidently been rehearsed, at least in part, and it was probably necessary to approach and locate this man beforehand as we learn that he doesn't like visitors. Moreover, let us not forget that Doc is a massive, tired, sometimes aging body. He always carries a briefcase, a backpack and announces his wish at the end of *Route One*, to end his trip by settling down and using his skills to help his compatriots.

Kramer explains in interviews that the people he meets during his trip know that he is not a doctor.[13] The tale is thus presented and accepted as such by the inhabitants of Route 1 who incidentally talk with the invisible character of Robert. He is the one who sees and hears people speaking, a narrating traveller who is brought into the conversation but who above all is a witness and unlike Doc does not practise participatory observation. He shares his vision with Doc but keeps a certain distance, so much so that he cannot logically understand the same thing or, it goes without saying, feel the same emotions as him. Sometimes Doc remains absent from view for a long time. What do we see then? Just about what he would see, or something totally different that he hasn't seen or that he won't see because quite simply he was absent. Indeed, we can fully accept that companions separate from time to time - this in fact becomes a theme of the second part of the film, when Doc decides to abandon the road [*Part Two*, 1:12].[14] At that point the tour operator takes over and heads the enquiry while the spectator can blissfully forget the filming mechanism adopted and appreciate the film as a documentary adopting a subjective point of view, which it is on several levels.

---

[12] "It's possible for example that Paul is busy [...] and that I'm 100 metres away busy filming something else. The sound engineer will say: "Paul is having an interesting conversation," because he listens with one ear and registers or doesn't register accordingly" *Points de départ*, (*op. cit.*, 78).

[13] For example, in a video recording with Octavia de Larroche (1994) available at the following address: http://derives.tv/entretien-video-avec-robert-kramer/ [consulted 15/03/22], 01:02.

[14] Kramer does however find Doc again, living in Miami at the end of the film [*Part Two*, 01:43].

This hesitation between reference and fictional systems is again reinforced by a series of images which do not emerge from a particular point of view. They seem to come from an omniscient camera disappearing behind its objective by hiding enunciative statements in order to tend towards a form of objectivity. The many perspectives certainly contribute to a questioning of the documentary's codes but above all they point to a territorial investigation taking into account all approaches to reality, which doesn't exist outside of us but according to a process put in place to question it.[15] Route 1 is diverse, enigmatic and changing. It can only be approached subtly and without imposing a confrontational or monolithic system. Kramer has made the choice of a type of improvisation: both a prewritten scenario and a stable type of filmic statement are out of the question. It is probably thanks to this approach, neither intrusive nor rigid, that the road is able to reveal some of its secrets.

## Tracks and trails

A finger, shot in closeup at the beginning of the film [*Part One*, 00:02], follows the outline of the road on a map,[16] from the Canadian border in Maine to Key West in Florida. The road is first and foremost just that, a path linking one point to another by entering the countryside in an abrupt way.[17] It is divided between various users who travel it as well as goods carted on it so it lends itself to an exchange of ideas or becomes the setting for cultural and social conflicts.[18] The road we are interested in crosses a space where more than a third of the country's population lives. It was the track for

---

[15] This updating of reality as a product of the enquiry is not subject to a "willing suspension of disbelief". François Niney rightly observed concerning a sequence filmed in an abortion clinic that "The fact that Doc isn't a real doctor, or a real reporter but an actor doesn't change anything about the reality of the scene" *L'Épreuve du réel à l'écran. Essai sur le principe de réalité documentaire*, (Brussels: De Boeck, "Art et cinéma," 2011 [2002]), 311.

[16] "[...] the first movement of the film is that of a finger filmed in close-up following Route 1 on a road map, from its beginning, at the border with Canada to its end, in Key West" (Gilles Chamerois, "Aller, revenir, tisser un abri: *Route One/USA* de Robert Kramer, 1989," (*Transatlantica*, 2012/2), 1.

[17] The road breaks the natural order through land-clearing, the filling in of wetlands, levees, tunnels, viaducts, etc." (Odon Vallet, "Le routard et la routine", (*Les Cahiers de médiologie*, 1996/2), 34.

[18] "[...] the conflicts for the use of roads are battles of competing economic orders, social classes, but also of values, of modernity, speed, displacement, uprooting" (Catherine Bertho-Lavenir, "Lutte de classes et d'influence," (*Les Cahiers de médiologie*, 1996/2), p. 140.

Indians then for the mail, the busiest axis in the USA until it came into competition with a highway, that is to say a communication channel which does not lend itself to the discovery of somewhere else or chance meetings (except if it is diverted from its first function).[19] Following the road is thus a way of covering all of its history, that of its settlement including finding oneself confronted by different groups of people and adapting to very different types of scenery, even if the centre of gravity in the film is undoubtedly between Boston and Washington. It is the "1000-km city" Kramer and his team cross through for two months.

This journey of course includes sites of remembrance, like the Vietnam Wall or Thoreau's reconstituted cabin. We understand that Kramer's camera turns away from oddities that a conscientious tourist would want to collect. The examples point to a selection process presiding over the choice of outstanding sites. The long passage given to the Washington Memorial should be related to the military past of both the filmmaker and Paul: the radical left in the USA was structured around a refusal of the Vietnam War. Thoreau's well-known cabin allows the film to evoke the disciple of civil disobedience and his fight against slavery (fighting side by side with "minorities" who are well represented in *Route One*, being the other component of military action of American youth threatening the *American Way of Life*). The filmmaker portrays other more intimate memories: his father's house evokes the history of emigration, and that of the bomb (his father, a doctor, was tasked with studying the effects of the explosion of the atomic bomb). His personal history intersects with major history: thus the "monument," desacralised because it is connected to personal journeys, is included in the film.

More often the filmmaker draws our attention to humbler things: an Indian basket skilfully woven that allows us to resuscitate a past slowly slipping into oblivion or a children's book (ordered at the New York Public Library whilst a pilgrimage follows to the little red lighthouse on the edge of the Hudson River underneath Washington Bridge which inspired this picture book). Another example is Monopoly pieces mass-produced by workers who will never get rich thanks to speculation on real estate. The road is also

---

[19] As it is the case in a study by Carol Dunlop and Julio Cortázar, *Les Autonautes de la cosmoroute ou un voyage intemporel Paris Marseille*, (Paris: Gallimard, NRF, "Du monde entire," 1983) -- Cortázar's texts translated by Laure Guille-Bataillon. The two travellers spend a month on the highway between Paris and Marseille, in their Volkswagen Combi, stopping "in the 65 parking lots on the highway at the rate of two per day." 15.

the story of the professions and activities which gave birth to it, made it increase in power, and then lose its attractiveness as the USA moved towards a post-industrial economy. Kramer films the world of work, that of lumbermen, fishermen, workers in the manufacturing industry... However, his film bears witness to the end of an era: from here on in, educators of all types (we can choose to call them social workers, teachers or policemen) accompany for better or worse the working class without factories or land, trying to survive in a devastated economic space.

Kramer is effectively interested in people. The road assigns them a place, geographically, culturally and economically speaking. Seeing this film above all means being confronted by communities who have their own codes and common ways of thinking, seeing and feeling. The filmmaker is never condescending even when he is confronted with ideologies he fights against (like at the beginning of the film, with the anti-abortion and anti-communist Christians who are right wing Republicans). From a privileged standpoint, he undeniably joins the fight with those who fall outside the mould of Reagan's America but he is always *with* those in front of the camera. The interview carried out with the colonel from a military base revelling in the fact that young people of the 80s had buried the dissenting ideals of their elders is an excellent example of this [*Part Two*, 00:58]. It is not the first take, as is shown by the voice-over: contact with this representative of an aggressive America sure of itself is apparently not immediate. Having said that, the film neither comments on nor attempts to control the interpretation of what is said. The filmmaker has the grace (it would be better to talk about ethics) to allow people and images to speak. To counterbalance this, the footage that captures progressive opinions is possibly not without irony. We can think of those portraying the nomination of Jesse Jackson, the Democrats' presidential candidate in 1984 and 1988, as a black dignitary.

Kramer's road is a space made up of many stories, that of the country, people who have settled there and of the one filming it. It's understood that every trip is completed in time, if only we reason in terms of duration related to travel, sensed and thematicised by a presenter transformed by this experience. Nevertheless, in our example, we see a road that is like the living conservatory of an America in turmoil, remembering its past and wondering about a conflictual future. From Maine to Florida, the territory extends over 5000 km, but the road says something more than a succession of landscapes leading from the northern forests to the Florida coastline via the megalopolis. The geographical layout is replaced or superimposed by a plethora of trails left, being made now or in the future, by those living (and often surviving) along Route 1.

## Disorientations

We could expect the trip to give a coherent vision of Kramer's America. Conditions seem fulfilled for an articulate discourse on this territory. This is in part what happens: the documentary sequences portray a sick country subjected to diverse forms of violence (ecological, economic, racial, sexual, etc.). *Route One* records the militant past of its director, within a movement, the *Newsreel,*[20] which considered film as a form of political activism. At the same time, and this is not necessarily contradictory, what dominates our vision during the film is chaos, a shattered and fragmented reality resisting the devil of interpretation. The poetics of the film are largely responsible for this state of affairs: Kramer refuses the very idea of a script (as do many documentarians including Wiseman),[21] highlights the diversity of points of view in logical sequence, sees the road as a catalogue of situations rather than a continuum, accepts improvisation, which is facilitated by the use of limited equipment for sound and image recording. We thus find ourselves faced with a *free* aesthetic "score" (jazz references are constant in Kramer's remarks; what's more he entrusted the composition of the soundtrack to Barre Philips). At the very end of the documentary the film, up till then organised in clearly identifiable and developed sequences (a giant bingo game on an Indian reservation, an ultra-conservative Protestant gathering, the Bridgeport ghetto, a wedding in the Hispanic community, etc.), accelerates, as if the camera "was running after", without attaining, a multifaceted and transient reality.

More generally, this road which should turn into a street at the entrance to a town, (but it isn't always possible to know when it starts or finishes), defines a strip along which urbanisation appears archaic, as is a landscape which does not correspond to the countryside or to nature. When nature does appear, it takes on a flourishing, rhizomatic form, like the mangroves in Florida or coral. The major impression is that of partially illegible space, buried under a multitude of clashing signs without any organising syntax. The film photography [see for example *Part One*, 00:28] which struggles to constitute a landscape, makes this chaos particularly visible. The shots

---

[20] The movement's manifesto is reproduced in *Points de départ*, (*op. cit.*, 27-28).
[21] Frederick Wiseman rightly underlines the importance of editing work in the making of his documentary which doesn't follow any established guiding principle: [...] the film is finished when after editing I have discovered the "script," *L 'Œuvre de Frederick Wiseman*, Vol. 1/1967 - 1979, (Paris: Blaq out, 2015), livret de présentation, 8.

follow one after another with no apparent logic, their scale varies; it appears that the image has no centre or vanishing point or guidelines focussing our attention. It is the same for people and their activities which occur at a rapid pace (people work a lot in *Route One*) but it is difficult to know what purpose this restlessness serves, or the teachings we could glean from the almost uninterrupted speech. Is this how people live? Between soup kitchens and charity balls, in abandoned cities, whilst politicians talk of hypothetical plans for urbanisation and public institutions, whilst city centres are deserted by the middle and upper classes. The journey into the past which we considered earlier is doubled by a revelation of the present whose keyword could be "disintegration": disintegration of the urban fabric, of social relationships, of political ideals. We would probably have to be partly foreign to this situation to be able to perceive it with such sharpness. Kramer confirms that he spent his youth without ever going further than 20 miles from Route One. He used to know it absolutely but no longer *recognizes* it after a ten-year period of exile. This is how you realize that people and things change when we have not seen them for a long period.

A final element reinforces the film's sense of loss of direction. Doc and Robert often play truant, by necessity or through choice (and what's more do not always find each other at the same place). We can effectively understand that it is not possible to take Route One for the whole trip (as we could do on a hiking trail or a country road): certain portions are in fact off limits for pedestrians, others are lost in the labyrinth of urban roads, still others have been downgraded or modified in terms of their course. Obviously, a road lives and is transformed, and while it is *almost* possible to follow it, (which Kramer did during the reconnaissance phase, travelling in his car from North to South), its use is not that of a highway linking seamlessly point A to point B. If finally, we take into account the nature of this enterprise (going to meet Americans and listening to them) and the attraction of peripheries for the film's protagonists, we will easily understand that there is nothing systematic or completely programmed on this trip. The direction to take is given but we can linger or go astray if it is worth the effort. If such had been the filmmaker's intent, editing and more intrusive comments could have led to a slightly more ordered chaos. Let us consider a short extract from Kramer given during a long interview with Bernard Eisenschitz:

> [...] we get to the middle of something, and so many components are given to you. It's fragmentary, chaotic, you will receive a lot of signs, lots of little things with which you will have to cope. I think it is a very faithful reflection

of the functioning of my mind.[22]

Kramer manages a considerable feat consisting in unsettling his spectator while at the same time driving him from beginning to end of his film on the same road, or nearly. This is the angle he has chosen to speak of his America.

The road crosses the country but also defines its identity or, more exactly, its identities. The one chosen by Kramer to put into words and images is of course emblematic. It continues to carry the number 1 referring to its origin and establishing a hierarchy which could aspire to the envied title of mother of all roads.[23] Situated along the coast, which saw the birth of a new country, marking the signs of the past along the journey, crossing centres of power, gathering together a considerable portion of the entire US population…it is part of those exceptional roads showcased for example by the *Guide du Routard* (even if it is in stiff competition in our contemporaries' imagination with its sister in the West, -- the *California State Route One* --, with *Route 66* or again with *Highway 61*). The filmmaker deconstructs this myth. This could be, if we wanted it to be, the controversial aspect of the film. However, it does not stop at denunciation. His film is generous because he knows how to listen to those living on the road without judging them, and looking at unremarkable places or so they appear at first sight. To sum up, he achieves the restoration and revival of a downgraded road (for the benefit of an "anti-road")[24] to represent an entire country. The film is entitled *Route One / USA*. It could have been called *Route One: USA*.

(Translated by Leisha ASHDOWN-LECOINTRE)

---

[22] *Points de départ* (*op. cit.*, 48).

[23] "The number 1 indicates the benchmark, the measure, the root irrigating the whole country. It also heralds as a primitive entity (the first number), a homecoming, a return to founding myths, to the freshness of first promises, to a unified dream before the division (the fork). "Being on the road" also means going back in time as we go ahead in space. Thus, throughout the trip, Kramer confronts these figures harking back to the origin of the USA and surviving in the form of commemorative monuments, conservatories, of observers and other descendents: the American Indians and the remains of their culture, George Washington and the Constitution, the Wars of Independence, slavery and its abolition" Mathieu Macheret, "What's up, Doc?," (*Critikat,* https://www.critikat.com/panorama/analyse/route-one-u-s-a/) [consulted on 19/03/2022].

[24] That is to say a highway. On this point, see François Dagognet, "Route, anti-route et méta-route" (*Les Cahiers de médiologie*, 1996/2), 19-28.

# Bibliography

Baldasari, Anne. "La photographie, la route, le territoire. Introduction aux paysages véhiculaires." *Cahiers de la photographie*, no. 14, *Le Territoire*, 1984

Bertho-Lavenir, Catherine. "Lutte de classes et d'influence." *Les Cahiers de médiologie*, 1996/2, 131-140

Boué, Caroline. "L'identité en marche dans *Route One USA* de Robert Kramer." *Tumultes*, no. 10, April 1998, 241-57

Chamerois, Gilles. "Aller, revenir, tisser un abri: *Route One/USA* de Robert Kramer, 1989." (*Transatlantica*, 2012/2), 1. https://doi.org/10.4000/transatlantica.6010

Dagognet, François. "Route, anti-route et méta-route." *Les Cahiers de médiologie*, 1996/2, 19-28

Daney, Serge. Entretien sonore entre Robert Kramer et Serge Daney, (1989), http://derives.tv/entretien-sonore-entre-robert-kramer-et-serge-daney/

de Larroche, Octavia. "Entretien vidéo avec Robert Kramer" 1994, http://derives.tv/entretien-video-avec-robert-kramer/

Dunlop, Carol and Julio Cortázar. *Les Autonautes de la cosmoroute ou un voyage intemporel Paris Marseille*, Paris: Gallimard, NRF, "Du monde entier." 1983

Eisenschitz, Bernard. *Points de départ. Entretien avec Robert Kramer*, Aix-en-Provence; Institut de l'Image, 2001

Euvrard, Jeanine. "Entretien avec Robert Kramer." *24 Images*, no. 92, 1998, 30-35

Gantheret, Lise. "L'énonciation personnelle du film." *Cahiers Louis-Lumière*, no. 8, 2011, 100-118

Macheret, Mathieu. "What's up, Doc?." *Critikat,* https://www.critikat.com/panorama/analyse/route-one-u-s-a/

David Martens. "Qu'est-ce que le portrait de pays ? Esquisse de physionomie d'un genre mineur." *Poétique*, Number 184, 2018/2, 247-268

Niney, François. *L'Épreuve du réel à l'écran. Essai sur le principe de réalité documentaire*, Brussels: De Boeck, "Art et cinéma." 2011 [2002]

Vallet, Odon. "Le routard et la routine," *Les Cahiers de médiologie*, 1996/2, 33-35

Wiseman, Frederick. *L'Œuvre de Frederick Wiseman*, Vol. 1/1967 – 1979

*Route one / USA*, directed by Robert Kramer, Les Films d'Ici / La Sept Paris, 1989, 255 min

# CHAPTER THREE

# "(…) THE ROAD AND ITS TURNINGS (…)": ROADSCAPES IN MOVIES AND VISUAL ART

## LAMBERT BARTHÉLÉMY

> (…) more than anything, it is the road and its turnings that is the traveler (…).
>
> —Robert Creeley, *Poem for Beginners*

In this contribution, I would like to consider some heterogeneous material made up of road films chosen in a denationalized and deperiodized corpus, but also of journeys of photographers (Depardon, Franck, Plossu, Lund) which, by the sequence of images collected, are never far from cinematographic scrolling. To this I will add artistic works, gleaned from the production of the last decades and which represent the road, or make the crossing of a distance their subject as well as their tool for elaboration (Fulton, Alÿs, Stalker). I will also underline some aspects of the imaginary of displacement that unfolds in the culture of the past half-century, to indicate certain issues, dynamics and values that support it.

This large and loose gathering of art works indicates clearly that I do not situate the road movie in a specific generic, national and temporal framework – that of the United States, the counterculture of the seventies and the complicated aftermath of the Western genre to put it succinctly. I consider it a hybrid, malleable and transcontinental narrative form that engages us to reflect on the changes that have affected the perception of reality and identity in recent decades. To put it another way, the road movie does not exist alone; nor does it exist so much in a particular place and time, as at the same time between different places. Without over-simplifying or neglecting the variety of possible configurations, we will try to determine what there can be in common in the articulation of a work of creation to the road as space-in-itself. This needs to be done independently of the forms that it is likely to take, royal or vernacular, highway or serpentine, and of the projects it supports. It seems to me that we can take the destabilization of identities, the percolations of the intercultural and the pollination of meaning characteristic of late capitalist societies, for the common denominator of the works which make displacement their determining issue. They constitute an experience of remembering, evaluation and remediation. In contemporary creation, the road appears as one of the ways to explore and respond to this general crisis of sensitivity. It is a way of deconstructing identities by systematically playing the logic of being against that of having, the contingent against the necessary, the peripheral against the central, to provoke a moral, ontological and cultural decentering of the subject. This makes the very decentering process valid in itself, and to which no explicit term is really assigned. Six films in chronological order, *The Rain People* (Francis Ford Coppola, 1969), *Five Easy Pieces* (Bob Rafelson, 1970), *Scarecrow* (Jerry Schatzberg, 1973), *Im Laufe der Zeit* (Wim Wenders, 1976), *Messidor*[1] (Alain Tanner, 1979) and *The Brown Bunny* (Vincent Gallo, 2003) as well as other examples, will support my argument. Now I simply would like to point out a few decisive operators of this research question.

The first and most obvious of these operators is the desire to *reinvent space*, which is reflected in the systematic questioning of the very notion of *limit*. These films all focus more on the journey than the final destination, more on the trespassing than the anchoring, even when it nevertheless seems that there is one goal *a priori* (as in *Scarecrow*, *Alice in den Städten* (Wim Wenders, 1974)*, Landscape in the mist*, (Theodoros Angelopoulos, 1988). The contemporary imagery of the road redefines the relationship that the subject develops with space, which is expressed mainly through the figures of detour, transit and immersion. Independently of its forms of actualization, this redefinition substitutes a relational vision for the territorial vision which dominates the representations of modernity.[2]

What spatial structures, what types of relationships with space configure the works that have itinerancy as an issue? Overall, these relationships of

---

[1] A European film which precedes feminine road cinema by ten years, of which Ridley Scott's *Thelma & Louise* (1991) is usually taken as the first manifestation.
[2] The crisis of the Western, which is usually linked to the emergence of the road movie, can be understood simply from this substitution, because the Western is by definition a territorial genre. Furthermore, the idea of a "spatial turn" as an interdisciplinary phenomenon in the social sciences was first articulated in 1989 by Californian geographer Edward Soja in his essay *Postmodern Geographies* (Verso, 1989).

disposition and proximity are non-metric, non-socialized, non-instrumental. Forms of smoothing the striated, produce smoothness within the striated, to use the categories developed by Deleuze and Guattari in *Mille Plateaux*. [3] Wandering, transit, drifting: so many ways of naming this disposition of the subject to the expanse, to the surfaces and to the open. This has little to do with the idea of travel (and its logic of securing identity through returning home), but rather aims to transcend the regimented spatial experience that constitutes the lot of the hypermodern subject. It is less a question of denying the historical and semiological closure of space, than of rendering it intermittently, temporarily, inoperative in order to confuse, hack, or incise it. This is what the marches organized by the Stalker collective since the 1990s aim at, or those initiated by Laurent Malone: to produce another shaping of space, which comes to be superimposed, during transit, on the dense agglomeration of the city and makes it possible to question its daily acceptance. [4] What I would like to call a road-work for convenience sake, does not necessarily invite its audience to escape from the techno-administered universe to remedy the overwhelming feeling of derealization. It encourages the audience on the other hand to modify its perceptual frameworks from within, to see and feel differently, and to re-consider its own ability to apprehend space. By being concerned with scale, proportion and points of view, by loosening the narrative fabrics, the work creates gaps for the contemporary subject, accustomed to low amplitudes of differentiation and to an obsessive filling of space. Its status borders on that of a pure utopian moment – not a systemic, collective and organized utopia. It is less the idea of another world, than that of a counter-exploration, or counter-factual exploration, of the world; less the idea of an elsewhere than the idea of an otherwise, of a differential practice. It is a bit like the temporary, ephemeral and moving zones of autonomy that Hakim Bey

---

[3] Gilles Deleuze & Félix Guattari, *Mille Plateaux* (Paris: Éd. de Minuit, 1980).

[4] In 1995, from October 5 to 8, for four days and three nights, the Stalkers toured Rome through the wastelands, interstitial and abandoned areas of the city. In January 1996, they followed two routes through the abandoned areas of the Milanese outskirts. In April of the same year, they tried a similar experience by leaving Paris from La Flèche d'Or, a former station of the ring road converted into a bar and a concert hall. They passed by the "peaches walls" of Montreuil to walk to Charles-de-Gaulle airport. In 2009 they produced Primavera Romana, a work consisting of a series of long walks, once or twice a week during the three spring months, which served to explore in stages the areas near the ring road that surrounds Rome. From Laurent Malone, we remember two urban crossing projects, the "JFK project," carried out in collaboration with Dennis Adam in 1997, and the Transects project carried out in Marseille in 2001.

could imagine in the 90s.[5] In a road movie nothing is ever really done with space, be it urban or natural. No one ever builds it. The traveling nomads frequent it and it has an effect on them – hypnotizes them, often.

The opening of *Gerry* (2002) by Gus Van Sant perfectly illustrates the idea of the deposition of the subject to and by space: we follow a pure, serene, and luminous road there, until it leaves us, literally, right in the middle of nowhere. We are left there for the rest of the film. No more normativity, no more beacons, no more rules, no more history, no more names – not even Paris, Texas: an absolute and general crisis of representation. In reality, it seems that every road movie, every road photograph, every artistic praxis related to travel, in one way or another undermines the very functionality of the road and its normative narrative. The road is demobilized from the use for which it is designed and told – social, economic, political, military use. The road is a site where points are connected and where knots and centers are created. It is where space is re-organized in a way that facilitates its possession and representation, allowing the exercise of authority. It always serves a goal, let us say the interests of the determined. It is there to be the rational instrument of the transformation of the landscape and the means of its integration, its humanization, also the warrant of its continuity, of its order and its security. But the road-work discards these functions. It is no longer a question of it in *Two Lane Blacktop*, which treats the American road as a space entirely defunctionalized and stripped of its narrative dynamics, totally available to play, to the sumptuous consumption of energy, to the mechanic (more than messianic) impulse, with no other purpose than itself. The road is burning energy, sending back a figure of absurd consumption to the triumphing consumer society, as a slap in the face of the economic market. It is as if all politics of the road suddenly vanished from the American horizon, as if it no longer guaranteed anything, to the point where the indeterminate invades the frame and ends up consuming it. What then is the road when it no longer serves a purpose or a power? It is a pure plane of immanence. What does a road do when it stops helping to culturalize the space? In a sense, it renaturalizes it, requalifies it for itself. By this I mean that it fights against its rationalization by providing us with an environmental experience that is hard to conceptualize: that of being in space in all contingency, without any need or capacity for hierarchical organization. It is as if it suddenly turned the implicit anthropocentrism of our representations against ourselves, or that it rather switches from the status of instrument *par excellence* of anthropocentrism to that of reverting to a nature-based relationship to the world. The road

---

[5] Hakim Bey, *TAZ. Temporary Autonomous Zone* (Autonomedia, 1991).

mobilized by contemporary art appears as the figure of an absolute change of scenery, of an indexing of the subject on the space and not of the space on the subject. That is to be incapable of finding one's way, to abandon oneself to an indeterminate position because of an excess of possible directions, to end up being indistinguishable in extension – as in *Entrare nell 'opera* (1971), a photograph by Giovanni Anselmo – or to recognize that representation is not commensurable with experience.[6]

Deculturalising the road, as carried out by recent art and fiction, is concomitant with the project of re-organizing our vision, because we still do not know how to see the world. Displacement always functions as a landscape revealer, as a stimulation of visual perceptions, as a means of a more intense exploration of the visible. Whatever the specific form of the space within which the movement takes place – be it exalting or deceptive, extra- or infra-ordinary, flat and emphatic or interstitial, humble, vulnerable and indecisive – we browse through many Third Landscapes.[7] We have a similar experience for instance in the *Monuments of Passaic* by Robert Smithson[8] or the "trespa-crossings" of the Stalker collective – they are always the object of an elementary attention which strives to reveal the quality(ies) of the marginal landscape. To allow the viewer to see them, revealing doesn't mean revealing the hidden, the secret or the forbidden, nor is it highlighting only cultural exaltation. It means the free sliding gaze over the surfaces that constitute the world and the experience of any singularity of space; it means that the eye grasps the transient, the fleeting, it locates and collects the imperceptible, the textures, the nebulosities. In short, it increases the emotional values of the territories.

---

[6] See Hamish Fulton, *An Object Cannot Compete With an Experience* (2001).

[7] Gilles Clément, *Manifeste du Tiers paysage* (Sujet/Objet éditions, 2007), 12 : "Si l'on cesse de regarder le paysage comme l'objet d'une industrie on découvre subitement (…) une quantité d'espaces indécis, dépourvus de fonction sur lesquels il est difficile de porter un nom. Cet ensemble (…) se situe aux marges. En lisière de bois, le long des routes et des rivières, dans les recoins oubliés de la culture, là où les machines ne passent pas. (…) Entre ces fragments de paysage aucune similitude de forme. Un seul point commun : tous constituent un territoire de refuge à la diversité. (…) Cela justifie de les rassembler sous un terme unique. Je propose Tiers paysage (…)." These landscapes are also present in *Wanda* (Barbara Loden, 1970), *Radio On* (Chris Petit, 1979), *Stranger than Paradise* (Jim Jarmusch, 1984) and *Landscape in the Mist*.

[8] A parody of a scenic excursion, *A Tour of the Monuments of Passaic, New Jersey* (narrative and photographs) appeared in *Artforum* in December 1967.

Fundamentally, the road has to do with this hypnotic capture of reality. It reveals the space, educates the eye of those who walk or drive by making it available, by detaching the gaze from any imperative of utility. What do we see when we look without intention? What is there, simply close, but not perceived as long as the gaze remains compartmentalized and polarized by utilitarian logics? Thus, the disarticulation of culturalized forms of apprehending space goes hand in hand with a ritual purging of the gaze (seeing what is there for what it is), a way of ordering the real independently from any subjective project, but with a deep feeling of commitment to the phenomenal intensities of things. [9] This way of letting space be, of disobjectifying it, of making it fluid, of letting things happen, echoes Emerson's idea of the transparent eye, [10] an eye which would be a pure surface of affect and would allow the implementation of a simple but radical optical democracy. That is to say a non-perspectivist, non-hierarchical, non-ordered perception of the world, an egalitarian perception of all the elements, animate or inanimate, which constitute it, a perception which is likely to give the impression that the landscape gazes at man, at least as much as it is gazed at by man. The landscape speaks of and for itself, tells itself, ultimately, all by itself. It is perhaps not entirely by chance that the road movie uses so many pan shots: they intentionally equate the human subject with the material of the world.

If the contemporary imagery of the road is primarily based on this attempt at a utopian requalification of spatial sense and of the gaze, it also involves unconventional experiences of temporality, close to what Raymond Depardon has labeled the downbeats[11] – and which can also be described as forms of suspension. They are a time in between, an empty form of present, a mere translation. The road movie also explicitly deals with the temporal off-screen of classic cinema. It tends to deviate from the strong beat logic and cares about what lies in between event nodes. This suspended temporality of the road takes on several figures: loop, rhizome, stratified, interpolation are some of the heterochronic hypotheses tested by drifters, road runners or walking artists. These hypotheses contrast with the temporal convention that governs our world, places it under a permanent emergency

---

[9] This is what Marc Rosmini perceives when he writes: "The road movie would therefore be a paradoxical genre which, at the same time, would disenchant and re-engage the world," in *Road Movies. 227 fragments sur un genre introuvable*, (Marseille: Images En Manœuvres Editions, 2012).

[10] Ralph Waldo Emerson, "Nature," in *Essais*, (Paris: Michel Houdiard, 1997), 16 ff.

[11] Raymond Depardon, "Temps faibles," *Errance*, (Paris: Seuil, 2000), 40.

regime and deprives it of any capacity for symbolization.[12] With the road, we leave the omnipotence of the chrony and we move towards Aion, towards a non-pulsed time, but which allows for this very reason a better integration of the conscious and the unconscious. We find the manifest gesture of this rupture, its *cliché*, in *Easy Rider* when Wyatt throws away his watch just before hitting the road. This means straightaway that the time on the road no longer has anything to do with the collective count, the quantity, the Promethean, the nodes of action, the eventful incandescence, the epic accelerations, that it is no longer subject to any "control procedure,"[13] but presents itself *a contrario* as pure expense. Expenditure as a temporal figure is very different from the ideology of "free time" which serves as a cover for the maximum saturation of work, since it is a question of occupying the liberated time, of filling it, to continue after all to consume it. From this point of view, time on the road is not free. This is not the time for tourism. It is unoccupied, unproductive, vacant. It is floating.

As we move forward in space, a complex, thick and strange temporality unfolds, forming a layer of the unactual taking on the appearance of a dream or a hallucination. Jean-Baptiste Thoret has described the specific time experience in road movies as a step back, coupling moving forward in space and regression in time.[14] As the journey confronts physical, even geological time, it also reconnects with psychic, mostly traumatic traces of the past. But road films speak probably more of spatio-temporal contamination, insofar as they expose a double becoming, the becoming-time of space, but also the becoming-space of time. It is an irradiated time, a time that has mutated, has branched out, whose indefinite process presents itself as a movement of dilation of the present. This makes it unactualized and within which the emotional strata combine, the affective flows combine, less to bring the subject back to itself, than to make it derive from itself. Anne Hurault-Paupe rightly remarks[15] that not much really happens in a road film,

---

[12] For a detailed construction of this concept and for the analysis of the forms and pathologies of temporality that accompany it, I refer to the work of Nicole Aubert, and in particular to her book *Le Culte de l'urgence . La société malade du temps* (Paris: Flammarion, 2003). See also the analysis of Jean-François Lyotard in "Le temps, aujourd'hui," in *L 'Inhumain. Causeries sur le temps* (Paris: Galilée, "débats", 1988).

[13] Jean-François Lyotard, *L 'Inhumain,* ibid p 85.

[14] Bernard Benoliel & Jean-Baptiste Thoret, *Road Movie, USA* (Paris: Hoëbeke, 2011).

[15] Anne Hurault-Paupe, "Le road movie : genre du voyage ou de l'Amérique immobile?" in René Gardies (ed.), *Cinéma et voyage*, (Paris: L'Harmattan Champs Visuels, 2007), 113-124.

that time is almost stagnant there, that it is as if suspended in inaction, even when a strong actantial tension supports the narrative *a priori*, as it does in *Bonnie & Clyde*. This is also generally the case in chase films, even when speed seems to prescribe the whole narrative, as in *Vanishing Point* (1971). At the end of the race, there is an ultimate suspension. Acceleration leads to satori: this is the paradox of the vanishing point, of the point of dissipation, that was already formulated in Kerouac's writings. What is in fact essential from the opening in Sarafian's film is less speed than a certain power of spectrality. That which the two contradictory endings tell – the one suggested by the (deleted) scene with Charlotte Rampling, in the role of a hitchhiker who is none other than death and the other that still occupies the three flashbacks punctuating the story. What happens in road films is that the amorphous duration generated by the journey opens up the way to an unrestrained flow of images, to their concatenation or their conflict, that it allows the return of confused, indecisive, diminished, often irreconcilable presences – of ghosts. These ghosts are of various natures: historical, affective, social, genealogical. They can call each other and mingle. We can identify the Ghost of America or of Germany, the Ghost of the father (*Landscape in the Mist*) or of the mother (as in Bergman's *Wild Strawberries*, 1957), the Ghost of the abandoned husband (*The Rain People*) or of a tragically lost love (*The Brown Bunny*) and finally the Ghost of the self (*Five Easy Pieces*) and the Ghost of Cinema (*Im Laufe der Zeit*). This is the paradox of the road: if the departure always has to do with a radical drop-out hope, a rupture, a release, the movement rather leads to engaging in dialogue with obsessions and dislocated feelings. The return of the ghosts also has the function of anchoring an ethical issue of the movement: to speak, to see again or to repair.

*The Brown Bunny* and *Im Laufe der Zeit* can serve as examples to illustrate this floating, out-of-date temporality that is set up on the road. However, the scale is not the same since Wenders' film is built around the discussion between personal and collective memory, while Gallo's gravitates around a purely intimate collapse of the main character, Bud Clay, caused by the accidental death (by overdose) of his former lover. Nevertheless, in both films, the road settles into an amorphous duration, within which the universes, both exterior and interior, the perceived and the mental, the asserted and the dreamed, quickly come to co-exist, and even merge in a form of imaginary space which saturates the consciousness of the character. Being on the road, *a fortiori* when the space is repetitive, uniform, minimal and abstract (desert), is to enter a time layer that functions like a transitional area: the relationship between presence and absence, lack and desire is constantly negotiated there,[16] subjective and objective, imaginary and real, here and elsewhere, self and other. This is a negotiation whose fiction does not necessarily intend to bring it to an end, preferring rather to expose the process, but which at least outlines the possibility, for the subject stuck in his neurosis, to neutralize the pain and to partly return to reality. This is what happens in Wenders' film at the end, when the two men separate, when the common journey is interrupted, when "everything has to be changed." However, what is meant by this – should we understand that nothing can stay the same? Considering that the self if inevitably altered by the other, is all identity imbricated? From another perspective, it is just the same premise in the film *Easy Rider*: if America cannot be found by Wyatt and Billy, then because it cannot be found as it is, this is because America has no united national body, no liberal and centered body, no pure, common and shared identity. The American identity that they seek exists only in the plural, only in the play on its fragmentations, infinitely divided, restless, contradictory and conflicting. Instead, they find borders and difference, less community than community-limit.

Contemporary nomadic artists have dealt with the question of temporality in a way that stimulates reflection. Whether they choose to walk in a natural environment or to drift in an urban context, they generally privilege processual figures of temporality (slowness; mutation; cycle), which function as utopian propositions and/or figures of reparation. Whatever the nature of the approach, it is always a question of arousing the emergence and collective awareness (spectator) of other forms, but also of other possible uses of temporality than those to which our contemporary situation forces us. They explore what we could overall call the temporal undersides of modernity, seek to unpack social time, to deconstruct it, to get it out of its regimentation by the imperatives of production. Many works produced over the last decades take the notion of evolution as a dynamic principle: working on scales of duration makes it possible to connect the divergent rhythms of human action and nature (for example the walking artists of the Seventies for which walking is the work – Fulton, Long, Tremlett, de Vries). Alternatively, they seek to catalyze transformations within the urban space, to generate dynamics of socio-geographical and relational evolution (archiving the temporal potential of abandoned urban territories, their power of perpetual change (Smithson, Stalker), to intervene concretely in the mutation of a social space, to create shared temporality), to travel in the past and the future of the city, through its forgotten memories and its unconscious becoming. Furthermore, they may reconnect through the

---

[16] See the cinematographic works of the American director, Vincent Gallo.

artistic proposal with natural anthropological time, or open up the way in which individuals are part of current time, to suggest to them another way of using time, less anxiety-provoking, less deadly – everything that points out circulation as a practice of resymbolization.

The last point I would like to address concerns the forms of subjectivity production that the road actualizes and the discourses of rupture that provide them with a conceptual background. The filmic, plastic or literary figuration of displacement systematically passes through a staging, more or less dramatized, more or less radicalized, of the exit, the breakaway or the escape. This is characterized by tearing away from symbolic orders and from social normativity, the crisis of belonging, pushing out of the institutional framework of art (land art) or cinema (New Wave, New Hollywood), *etc*. In short, it is defined as a shift, a decentering as a common denominator. The point of entry is always the transgression of frames and establishes the situation of the subject (or of the medium) in capitalist and patriarchal society (Natalie in *The Rain People*), of what gives (imposes?) a place, a role, a history, a genealogy, an identity, a domesticity, a routine. This defines it in a functional and permanent way, by a set of coordinates. Departure, uprooting, deviation: suddenly the protagonist is gone, has run away, has seceded. Or it can also happen that it is absent through an economic or legal process (losing a job, retirement, *etc*.) which deprives them of a position, forces them to glean, for example, rather than participate in the commercial circuit of goods (Agnès Varda, *Sans toit ni loi*). Notwithstanding, the subject/protagonist becomes in any case a figure of refusal and opposition: a Bartleby in motion; sand in the wheels; a ghost in the machine; an experimental subject. We can speak of a utopian subject, seeking to invent itself in and by the very uprooting and the operation of production of difference that this entails.[17] This subject does not come back either.

From this inaugural gesture of de-anchoring, the film, the novel, the plastic proposal undertake on the one hand to document its constitution in a form (or a style) of life (decentering, fluctuation, disorientation), to explore the alternative values it suggests. On the other hand, it proposes to examine the future of this opposition, to test its relevance or fragility, to assess its critical effectiveness with regard to the one-dimensionality of the contemporary world. It will thus be able to focus on its positive valence (liberation, desire,

---

[17] It is possible to see in this position of marginality the cause of the critical interest that the road film arouses: it offers a rather direct metaphor for the "displaced" condition of the intellectual in the contemporary world.

inventiveness…) – which is rather the position held by plastic productions and by certain films with a more factual dynamic, those of Patrick Keiller or Robert Kramer for instance; or to draw attention to its negative valence (loss, dislocation, dangers inherent in the process and which compromise the trajectory) – a position more resolutely held by fiction cinema. Or even articulate the two axes, in a perspective of profane catabasis (*Easy Rider, Into the Wild*: liberation gives way to alienation), or of anabasis (*Im Laufe der Zeit, Dead Man*: alienation gives way to liberation).

The staging of alternative, experimental, deterritorialized subjectivities (outlaw, solitary drifter, nomadic artist), distinct from those of emigration, the diaspora or exile (the three other spatial tropes commonly used to describe the uprooted condition of postmodern subjectivity),[18] constitutes the project that legitimizes bringing together the various artistic spaces. As I have summarily attempted to show, it should be noted, and this will be my provisional conclusion, that this legitimacy is reinforced by the observation that the questioning of alternative subjectivities is done from ontological rather than hermeneutic logic, and from relational scenarios rather than essentialist postulates. I mean that if identity (its flaws, its ruptures, its dissonances, *etc.*) is indeed the problematic driving force of most road-works, it is less the meaning that determines displacement, than the experimentation of protocols of existence rid of the question of origin. It is less a question of (re)finding oneself, than of replacing. This explains in particular the more or less systematic substitution of horizontal community figures for traditional connections of the vertical type. Because displacement dissolves the established forms of community (substance, identity or genealogy: couple, family, work, country, etc.), while bringing out, as in utopian counter-shots, various practices of impure community, where the common is no longer defined by a substantial and homogeneous identity, but by a differential activity, this activity is narrative. This constitutes neither accumulation, nor progression, nor synthesis but an assembling of local stories, of anecdotes. Narrative competence opens up the possibility of a community of relationship, which is "present in the pure event of its manifestation,"[19] which is about encounter and reciprocity, and whose content can never be anticipated, since it turns out to be determined by the

---

[18] The diaspora is always collective, and it does not necessarily imply the desire to return. Exile can be lonely, painful, and involves a desire to return.
[19] François Noudelmann, *Pour en finir avec la généalogie* (Léo Scheer, 2004), 166.

interplay of temporary subjective implications.[20] It is a modular community, with no assigned representational background, a community of declension and not of identification, or of essence, necessarily led to come apart, but also, and just as necessarily, to recompose itself, to reform itself in any place and at any time. From this point of view, it is a form of eternal community, superior to identity communities in that it does not derive its legitimacy from any form of violence, nor from any ideological shaping of reality, but from a peaceful gesture of consent to listen and to speak to the other. In another glossary, this is called an *alliance*. What finer figure of this than the character of GTO in the so-called mute *Two Lane Blacktop* (1971)! I believe this is one of the powerful elements to take into account in road movies, if one speculates on their apparent pessimism at the end. I would suggest that the important thing there is less the quest, which inevitably turns out to be deceptive, than the pluralization of the self through experience, which precedes the final (and brutal) interruption of the narrative, its unfinished business, more than its end. Now this pluralization, this potentiation, which is not the discovery of an authentic self, but the result of its participation in the contingency of the world, escapes any apparent reassertion of the law: end of *Zabriskie Point* (1970). It constitutes a witch line[21] and even after the end, preserves the voice of the irreconcilable at the heart of contemporary culture.

## Bibliography

Aubert, Nicole. *Le Culte de l'urgence. La société malade du temps*, Paris: Flammarion, 2003.

Benoliel, Bernard & Jean-Baptiste Thoret. *Road Movie, USA*, Paris: Hoëbeke, 2011.

Bey, Hakim. *TAZ. Temporary Autonomous Zone*, Autonomedia, 1991.

Clément, Gilles. *Manifeste du Tiers paysage*, Sujet/Objet éditions, 2007.

Deleuze, Gilles & Félix Guattari. *Mille Plateaux*, Paris: Éd. de Minuit, 1980.

Depardon, Raymond. "Temps faibles." *Errance*, Paris: Seuil, 2000.

Emerson, Ralph Waldo. "Nature." in *Essais*, Paris: Michel Houdiard, 1997.

---

[20] This kind of community is found in "docufictive" approaches à la Kramer (*Route One, USA*) or Varda (*La Glâneuse et les glâneurs*). Kramer, in particular, in the splendid *Route One*, is totally on it: finding the American people ravaged by the Reagan years, or at least reactivating their memory, goes through this staging of listening.

[21] Translation of Deleuze's "ligne de sorcière."

Fulton, Hamish. *An Object Cannot Compete With an Experience*. London: Sainsbury Centre for Visual Arts, 2001.

Hurault-Paupe, Anne. "Le road movie : genre du voyage ou de l'Amérique immobile ?." in René Gardies (ed.), *Cinéma et voyage*, Paris: L'Harmattan "Champs Visuels." 2007, 113-124.

Lyotard, Jean-François. in "Le temps, aujourd'hui." in *L'Inhumain. Causeries sur le temps*, Paris: Galilée, "débats." 1988.

Noudelmann, François. *Pour en finir avec la généalogie*, Léo Scheer, 2004.

Soja, Edward. *Postmodern Geographies. The Reassertion of Space in Critical Social Theory*. London, New York: Verso, 1989.

# Films

*Five Easy Pieces*, directed by Bob Rafelson, (1970, 98 min).

*Gerry*, directed by Gus Van Sant, (2002, 103 min).

*Im Laufe der Zeit*, directed by Wim Wenders, (1976, 176 min).

*Landscape in the Mist,* directed by Theo Angelopoulos, (1988, 127 min).

*Messidor*, directed by Alain Tanner, (1979, 123 min).

*Radio On*, directed by Chris Petit, (1979, 104 min).

*Sans toit ni loi*, directed by Agnès Varda, (1985, 106 min).

*Scarecrow*, directed by Jerry Schatzberg, (1973, 112 min).

*Stranger than Paradise*, directed by Jim Jarmusch, (1984, 89 min).

*The Brown Bunny*, directed by Vincent Gallo, (2003, 119 min).

*The Rain People*, directed by Francis Ford Coppola, (1969, 101 min).

*Wanda*, directed by Barbara Loden, (1970, 105 min).

# Chapter Four

## Applying Principles of Interpretation to Reveal Beauty and Meanings within Roadscapes

## Ted T. Cable

Marcel Proust wrote that the real voyage of discovery lies not in seeking new lands, but in seeing with new eyes.[1] This chapter will present the principles of heritage interpretation and their application to helping travelers see the notoriously mundane roadscapes along the U.S. Interstate Highway System with "new eyes." These roads and the associated agricultural landscapes have reputations for being monotonous, uninteresting, and something to be endured, rather than enjoyed. By applying heritage interpretation principles to reveal hidden beauty, tell inspirational stories, and make personal meanings, these books and scripts have been shown to transform the travel experience from dull and boring to engaging, entertaining and educational. This chapter proposes an interpretive approach to give travelers "new eyes" in which to perceive roadscapes. Examples will be drawn from a corpus of published travel books written by the author about traveling the high-speed cross-country Interstate highways through the central United States.

---

[1] The original French quotation is, "Le seul véritable voyage, le seul bain de Jouvence, ce ne serait pas d'aller vers de nouveaux paysages, mais d'avoir d'autres yeux, de voir l'univers avec les yeux d'un autre, de cent autres, de voir les cent univers que chacun d'eux voit, que chacun d'eux est." *À la Recherche du temps perdu*. Vol. 5 *La Prisonnière* (Paris: Gallimard, 1923), 69.

# The birth of the U.S. Interstate Highway System, a "military" roadscape

In 1956, U.S. President Eisenhower signed the Interstate Highway Act, creating the largest public works project in US history. In 1919 he had traveled across the United States from Washington, DC, to San Francisco on a convoy of army vehicles meant to test both the nation's roads and the vehicles that had been used in World War I. The results were not good. Most roads were dirt, bridges collapsed along the way, and vehicles constantly broke down. Eisenhower personally wrote the dismal trip report concluding that America's road system needed great improvement. Moreover, Eisenhower gained additional experience with roadways in Europe during World War II. Germany's *autobahn* moved military and civilian vehicles efficiently. This impressed upon Eisenhower the importance of having good highways to move military personnel and equipment; he also understood the importance of being able to evacuate cities quickly in the event of attack. In fact, one of the goals of the highway act was to link all cities having a population greater than 50,000 people. So, to a significant degree, interstate highways are an artifact of war and especially the Cold War with the Soviet Union. They were born out of the need for evacuations, not holiday vacations. With these purposes in mind, it is not surprising that at least in many regions of the United States Interstates are not known as routes with spectacular roadscapes. Their design promotes traveling as fast as possible and they strategically avoid mountains, hills, and river and lake crossings (due to the expense of bridge building) whenever possible which in turn leads to more monotonous landscapes. In fact, there exists a whole genre of American travel literature encouraging people to get off the Interstate highways and instead travel on the backroads of America. They admonish travelers to "get off the beaten path." The most famous and influential of these was the autobiographical travel book *Blue Highways: A Journey into America* by William Least Heat-Moon (1982).[2] The blue highways of the title refer to the lesser traveled roads that were often depicted in blue on road maps, whereas the main roads typically were red. This chapter presents an attempt to overcome the stereotype of interstate highway travel being boring and tedious. The goal was to make traveling Interstate highways more enjoyable, engaging and educational. To this end, we applied the principles of the profession of heritage interpretation.

---

[2] William Least Heat-Moon, *Blue Highways: A Journey into America* (New York: Fawcett Crest, 1982).

## Interpretation: Definitions and Principles

Heritage and nature interpretation as a formal profession probably began in the late 19th century in the Alps and then shortly thereafter in the Rocky Mountains of North America.[3] The classic definition of interpretation offered by Tilden (1957) states that interpretation is, "An educational activity which aims to reveal meanings and relationships through the use of original objects, by firsthand experience, and by illustrative media, rather than simply to communicate factual information."[4] Sam Ham captured much of the current thinking about what the term entails, "Interpretation is a mission-based approach to communication aimed at provoking in audiences the discovery of personal meaning and the forging of personal connections with things, places, people and concepts."[5] The U.S. State of Arkansas developed a succinct, yet powerful, definition which is used in their parks and historic sites: "Interpretation is communication that goes beyond facts to reveal what things mean, how they fit together, and why they matter."[6]

In the late 1950s, Freeman Tilden wrote intertwined and inspiring "principles of interpretation." Tilden's (1957) principles have stood the test of time, perhaps because of their lucidity, perhaps because of their inscrutability that rings with a sense of truth. These principles still serve as guidelines for performance, for evaluation, and for training. Box 1 presents Tilden's six principles. Building on the work of Tilden, Beck and Cable[7] developed an expanded and modernized set of interpretive principles. The first six principles are consistent with Tilden's although they have been updated. (see Box 2).

---

[3] Ted T. Cable and Catherine Morgan-Proux. "The nature guides of Chamonix." in *Legacy* 29 (5) 2018, 6-9.

[4] Freeman Tilden, *Interpreting our Heritage*. (Chapel Hill, NC: The University of North Carolina Press), 9

[5] Sam Ham, *Interpretation: Making a Difference on Purpose* (Golden, CO: Fulcrum Publishing, 2013)

[6] Kelly Farrell, "What is a park interpreter?" May 2017,
https://www.arkansasstateparks.com/articles/what-park-interpreter

[7] Larry Beck and Ted Cable, *The Gifts of Interpretation: Fifteen Guiding Principles for Interpreting Nature and Culture* (3rd ed.). (Urbana, IL: Sagamore Publishing, 2011)

## The challenge of finding beauty in "empty" or "cluttered" roadscapes

The application of interpretive principles to travel on U.S. Interstate highways took the form of three guidebooks: one each for the states of Kansas,[8] Missouri,[9] and Illinois.[10] These three books apply the interpretive principles to address different roadscape challenges in each state. In Kansas the roadscape is almost entirely rural with large sections of tallgrass prairie grasslands, semi-arid steppe, and cropland dominated by wheat fields. The lack of topography and trees creates immense open spaces and wide horizons along the route. In *Blue Highways: A Journey into America*, Least Heat-Moon describes the experience of driving through this landscape as follows:

> The true West differs from the East in one great, pervasive, influential, and awesome way: space. It's that apparent emptiness which makes matter look alone, exiled, and unconnected. Those spaces diminish man and reduce his blindness to the immensity of the universe; they push him toward a greater reliance on himself, and, at the same time, to a greater awareness of others and what they do. But, as space diminishes man and his constructions in a material fashion, it also--paradoxically--makes them more noticeable. Things show up out here. No one, not even the sojourner can escape the expanses. You can't get away from them by rolling up the safety-glass and speeding through, because the terrible distances eat up the speed. Still, drivers race along; but when you get down to it, they are people uneasy about space.[11]

The Illinois roadscape is an extremely flat terrain and largely agricultural with corn and soybeans being the primary crops. However, the route across Illinois is anchored at each end by large urban areas of St. Louis and Chicago. Moreover, near its midpoint the interstate goes through Springfield, the capital city of Illinois. Anecdotally, residents of the Chicago area often

---

[8] Ted T. Cable and Wayne A. Maley, *Driving across Kansas: A Guide to I-70.* Newly Revised and Updated Edition. (Lawrence, KS: University Press of Kansas, 2017).

[9] Ted T. Cable and L. Cadden, *Driving Across Missouri. A Guide to I-70* (Lawrence, KS: University Press of Kansas. 2010).

[10] LuAnne Cadden and Ted T. Cable, *Traveling Through Illinois: Stories of Landmarks and Landscapes between St. Louis and Chicago* (Charleston, SC: History Press/Arcadia Publishing, 2013)

[11] William Least Heat-Moon, *Blue Highways: A Journey into America* (New York: Back Bay Books, 1982), 132.

say that everything south of Cook County (the county where Chicago is located) is "nothing but corn."

The Missouri route is much more urban and congested. It travels through the large metropolitan areas of Kansas City, St. Louis, and Columbia. Between these cities there are areas of forest and agriculture. In these areas many advertising billboards line the highway. The tagline for promoting the guidebook to the interstate through Missouri became "See the beauty beyond the billboards!"

The challenge for these three books, in which the principles of interpretation were applied, was to find interesting landmarks and inspiring stories in the spacious, seemingly mundane, and sometimes cluttered roadscapes along these Interstate highways.

## Sparking an interest

In this section, selected principles of interpretation are presented along with examples of how each principle was applied. According to Tilden, to spark an interest, interpreters must relate the subject to the lives of the people in the audience. The interpretive messages must touch something in the personality or previous experiences of audience members, or it will be sterile.[12] Being able to relate to it implies that they must understand and be able to process the communication being offered to them. We applied this principle when interpreting a wetland along the highway, in the way we chose to explain its many benefits to local communities. To help the reader personally relate to the benefits of wetland functions they were compared to sponges and water filters, things with which readers are familiar. Wetlands "...serve as a natural sponge to soak up floodwaters and as nature's filter, removing pollutants. Wetlands also allow rains to replenish the groundwater rather than run off, a vital function out here on the Plains where people rely on the groundwater for irrigation and nearly all their water needs."[13]

## Revealing meaning and truth

Information is merely the raw material of interpretation. As Tilden's second principle states, the purpose of interpretation goes beyond providing

---

[12] Tilden, *op.cit.*, 9.
[13] LuAnne Cadden and Ted T. Cable, *op. cit.*, 96.

information to reveal deeper meaning and truth.[14] Those interpreting to audiences must not only give a series of facts such as dates or statistics, but must answer the question, "So what?" in the minds of the audience. The interpreter must answer the question why should my audience care about any of this? We apply this principle in a story about a wind energy farm. All the statistics regarding the wind turbines and megawatts of energy production are provided, but then we explain what this means in terms of household energy needs to answer the "so what?" question. For example, we state that, "Each tower stands 80 meters (265 feet) high and is topped by an electricity-generating turbine that is capable of producing 1.5 megawatts. At typical efficiencies, this is enough energy to supply the needs of 332 homes. This "farm" has 155 towers, meaning that, collectively, it could serve the needs of more than 50,000 households."[15]

## Storytelling that informs, entertains, and enlightens

People remember stories and are more likely to find them more engaging than simply a lecture or encyclopedic presentation. Great interpreters are great storytellers. As an example of storytelling as an interpretation principle in action, let us focus on the story behind a particular brick chimney that rises up just off the highway. It is now covered in vines and surrounded by brush. An old analog television antenna still extends from the top of the chimney, looking like a cross. It is likely that very few of the millions of people who drive by every year even notice it. And those that do undoubtedly quickly dismiss it. In interpreting this chimney, we add meaning to the chimney by telling the story of the woman who lived in the house. It burned to the ground as a result of an electrical problem. Our story explains how this changed her life, and that passing it each day is a reminder of what she lost but also a reminder of her resilience and strength to overcome that loss. These are all compelling elements of her story that evoke empathy and interest. We include part of her interview wherein she expressed deep emotion.

> This was the first, and only, home I have ever purchased. To lose the house was devastating, but more devastating was to lose the contents inside the home that can never be replaced—the pictures, yearbooks, childhood toys and family furniture. Those are the things I think about each time I drive past on I-70. To lose everything is hard to overcome and I still feel sad. Some

---

[14] "Information, as such is not Interpretation. Interpretation is revelation based on information." Tilden, *op. cit.*, 9.
[15] LuAnne Cadden and Ted T. Cable, *op. cit.*, 45.

day when I purchase another home I will take down the chimney and use the bricks to build a fire pit in the back yard."[16]

Our text goes on to present the story of how she rebuilt her life and moved on with a new appreciation for the things she has and a deeper sympathy for victims of disasters whose homes are destroyed. Through the use of story this nondescript and often ignored feature of the roadscape is now a meaningful symbol of loss and the determination to overcome it.

## Presenting a complete theme

Research has shown that people forget facts but remember themes.[17] An overarching theme threaded throughout the three travel books on the interstate highway I-70 is that "Farmers grow more than food." When interpreting the expansive cornfields and soybean fields along the highways, data is given about acreages and crop yields, but then to add deeper meaning (see the principle of revealing meaning and truth) we elaborate on the enormous variety of not only foods, but products which come from the crops. The following passage dealing with a cornfield illustrates our project of presenting a complete theme.

> About 60 percent of the U.S. corn crop is fed to livestock to become meat. When not fed to livestock a bushel can yield 32 pounds of cornstarch, 2.8 gallons of ethanol auto fuel, or 33 pounds of corn sweetener - a widely used sweetener in soda - enough to sweeten more than 400 cans of soda. More than 4200 supermarket products contain corn or corn by-products, including such unlikely items as toothpaste, salad dressings, chewing gum, peanut butter, aspirin, catsup, mustard, coffee and tea. Nonfood items that are made from corn include detergents, sandpaper, plastics, cosmetics, wallpaper, crayons, shoe polish, ink, fireworks, road de-icers and even tires. You may have corn products in your fuel tank and car tires right now![18]

## Sensing the beauty in our surroundings

Millions of travelers drive the interstate highways on their way to experience the spectacular beauty of mountains, lakes, seashores, forests as well as architectural and archeological wonders. As they focus on these destinations, the premise of our work is that they unknowingly pass by and miss beautiful vistas, landscapes, and objects whose beauty is more subtle

---

[16] Cable and Maley, *op. cit.*, 36
[17] Ham, *op. cit.*,13.
[18] Cable and Maley, 93.

and requires closer attention. Our primary goal in writing these books was to help people see beauty in things (and people) that are not superficially and obviously pretty. We were drawing on the principle that interpretation should instill in people the ability, and the desire, to sense the beauty in their surroundings—to provide spiritual uplift and to encourage resource preservation. The books reveal the beauty of such things as blades of grass, fertile soils, roadside birds and animals, swamps and marshes, unique fences, and the resourcefulness of people who lived on the land in the past. We called these things "mundane miracles" and hoped to reveal the miraculous beauty of common objects and scenes. An example of this principle can be found in the section we devoted to cemeteries. Travelers often pass by cemeteries without taking notice of them. A closer look reveals beauty among the graves. An excerpt dealing with one such cemetery demonstrates roadside beauty that is often missed by travelers.

> From 1870 to 1930, iron crosses were popular grave markers on the Great Plains from Canada to here in Kansas, particularly in Catholic cemeteries. The wrought iron was tough enough to withstand the winds, fires, blizzards, and prairie thunderstorms, and in this strength, they represented the strength and resilience of the settlers themselves. Crosses were made by local blacksmiths, many of whom learned the blacksmithing trade back in "the old country" of the Volga and Black Sea regions of Russia. Blacksmiths would vary their intricate designs to tell the story of the deceased without the use of words. The size, shape, color, and design of the wrought-iron crosses have personal and cultural significance. As blacksmithing became a lost art in the mid- to late twentieth century, marble, granite, and cement markers became more popular than iron crosses. Check out these historic pieces of folk art, and see if you can read the stories they tell of the people they honor.[19]

## Conclusion

The efforts to make driving on Interstate highways more enjoyable, engaging and educational seem to be successful. Widespread use of these three travel books, as measured by sales, indicate that travelers are prepared to question the narrative that the roadscapes of the mid-West are "empty" or boring, and to see them with new eyes that are open to an unsuspected kind of beauty. The belief that the books are worthwhile, and that there is significant market demand for them has led to the publisher wanting to publish more editions. Anecdotally, positive feedback in the form of letters, emails and phone calls from readers have demonstrated that the books are

---

[19] Cable and Cadden, *op. cit.*, 2013.

creating the desired effect. Indeed, the application of interpretative principles is making traveling through Interstate highway roadscapes in the United States more rewarding for travelers.

## Bibliography

Beck, Larry, & Ted T. Cable. *The Gifts of Interpretation: Fifteen Guiding Principles for Interpreting Nature and Culture* (3rd ed.). Urbana, IL: Sagamore Publishing, 2011.

Beck, Larry, Ted T. Cable and Douglas Knudson. *Interpreting Cultural and Natural Heritage: For a Better World.* Urbana, IL: Sagamore Publishing, 2018.

Cable, Ted T., and LuAnne Cadden. *Driving Across Missouri. A Guide to I-70.* Lawrence, KS: University Press of Kansas, 2010.

Cable, Ted T., and Wayne Maley. *Driving across Kansas: A Guide to I-70: Newly Revised and Updated Edition.* Lawrence, KS: University Press of Kansas, 2017.

Cable, Ted T., & Catherine Morgan-Proux. "The nature guides of Chamonix" *Legacy* 29 (5), 2018, 6-9.

Cadden, LuAnne and Ted T., Cable. *Traveling Through Illinois: Stories of Landmarks and Landscapes between St. Louis and Chicago.* Charleston, SC. History Press/Arcadia Publishing, 2013.

Ham, Sam. *Interpretation: Making a Difference on Purpose.* Golden, CO: Fulcrum Publishing, 2013.

Least Heat-Moon, William. *Blue Highways: A Journey into America.* New York: Fawcett Crest, 1982.

Tilden, Freeman, *Interpreting our Heritage.* Chapel Hill, NC: The University of North Carolina Press, 1957.

**Box 1. Tilden's Principles of Heritage Interpretation (Tilden, 1957)**

Tilden's Principles of Interpretation

I. Any interpretation that does not somehow relate what is being displayed or described to something within the personality or experience of the visitor will be sterile.

II. Information, as such, is not interpretation. Interpretation is revelation based upon information. But they are entirely different things. However, all interpretation includes information.

III. Interpretation is an art, which combines many arts, whether the materials presented are scientific, historical, or architectural. Any art is to some degree teachable.

IV. The chief aim of interpretation is not instruction, but provocation.

V. Interpretation should aim to present a whole rather than a part and must address itself to the whole person rather than any phase.

VI. Interpretation addressed to children should not be a dilution of the presentation to adults, but should follow a fundamentally different approach. To be at its best it will require a separate program.

**Box 2. A Further Developed Set of Interpretation Principles (Beck and Cable, 2011)**

1.  To spark an interest, interpreters must relate the subject to the lives of the people in the audience.

2.  The purpose of interpretation goes beyond providing information to reveal deeper meaning and truth.

3.  The interpretive presentation—as a work of art—should be designed as a story that informs, entertains, and enlightens.

4.  The purpose of the interpretive story is to inspire and provoke people to broaden their horizons.

5.  Interpretation should present a complete theme or thesis and address the whole person.

6.  Interpretation for children, teenagers, and seniors—when these comprise uniform groups—should follow fundamentally different approaches.

7.  Every place has a history. Interpreters can bring the past alive to make the present more enjoyable and the future more meaningful.

8.  Technology can reveal the world in exciting new ways. However, incorporating this technology into the interpretive program must be done with foresight and thoughtful care.

9.  Interpreters must concern themselves with the quantity and quality (selection and accuracy) of the information presented. Focused, well-researched interpretation will be more powerful than a longer discourse.

10. Before applying the arts in interpretation, the interpreter must be familiar with basic communication techniques. Quality interpretation depends on the interpreter's knowledge and skills, which must be continually developed over time.

11. Interpretive writing should address what readers would like to know, with the authority of wisdom and its accompanying humility and care.

12. The overall interpretive program must be capable of attracting support—financial, volunteer, political, administrative—whatever support is needed for the program to flourish.

13. Interpretation should instill in people the ability, and the desire, to sense the beauty in their surroundings—to provide spiritual uplift and to encourage resource preservation.

14. Interpreters can promote optimal experiences through intentional and thoughtful program and facility design.

15. Passion is the essential ingredient for powerful and effective interpretation—passion for the resource and for those people who come to be inspired by it.

# CHAPTER FIVE

# IS THE ROAD AMERICA(N)?
## JOHN STEINBECK'S *TRAVELS WITH CHARLEY.*
## *IN SEARCH OF AMERICA*

## ISABEL OLIVEIRA

In Paul Bowles' novel, *The Sheltering Sky* (1949), one of the characters, Porter Moresby, remarks that he does not see himself as a tourist but as a traveler and he tries to explain why:

> Whereas the tourist generally hurries back home at the end of a few weeks or months, the traveler, belonging no more to one place than to the next, moves slowly, over periods of years, from one part of the earth to another. … Another important difference between tourist and traveler is that the former accepts his own civilization without question; not so the traveler, who compares it with the others, and rejects those elements he finds not to his liking.[1]

The argument posits the impossibility of truly being or becoming a traveler since, at some point in time, even if it is years later, most individuals who travel eventually return to their place of origin, which is considered home. Consequently, it also suggests that most travel narratives are actually produced by tourists rather than genuine travelers. Finally, it proposes that a genuine traveler distinguishes their own culture from others, actively selecting which aspects to embrace or reject. We can examine John Steinbeck's travels throughout the United States to consider how both premises may apply.

The tourist/traveler debate is not exclusively contemporary but has been going on since the beginning of mass tourism. This phenomenon coincided with the technological advances in travel during the mid-nineteenth century

---

[1] Paul Bowles, *The Sheltering Sky* (London: Penguin Books, 2009 [1949]), 5-6.

in countries that were experiencing massive industrial development—a process in which the United States became particularly immersed after the end of the Civil War. This is the debate that distinguishes the attractive (and often romanticized and idealized) traveler from the unwanted (and not very romantic) hordes of tourists. The former was particularly attractive to Americans because of a strong belief in the self-awareness that could be acquired through traveling. After all, America was the result of many journeys, and the American territory was the stage for the most mythically famous of them all: going West.

If Americans were on the move, there was a corresponding interest in travel literature, which thrived in the United States, especially during the 19th century, as American readers sought to either plan their own journeys or indulge in pleasurable reading that would transport them vicariously. This surge in popularity coincided with the growing ease of Americans traveling to Europe, thanks to advancements in transportation.[2] Well-established British writers were the ones widely read, but Americans were eager to embrace a new type of travel writer—one that could give them an avowed American perspective. It makes sense that if travel accounts were to be made, one could not ignore the travelers who had preceded them, nor could they presume to ignore some established traditions of the genre. Being a composite literary form, travel literature has resisted categorization but at the end of the nineteenth century it did exhibit certain forms and conventions, which were being drawn up by every kind of writer, thus making redundancy inevitable. This was not a problem restricted to American writers since in "How to Write a Book of Travels" (1840) Frederick Marryat, who was a successful British travel writer himself, captures with comic overstatements the formulaic approaches to the genre when he puts Barnstable, a mentor, advising Ansard, the narrator, on how to write a travel book in the following way:

> Traveling – remarks on country passed through – anecdote – arrival at a town – churches – population– historical remarks – another anecdote – eating and drinking – natural curiosities – egotism – remarks on women (never mind the men) – another anecdote – reflections – an adventure – and go to bed.[3]

---

[2] See Alfred Bendixen and Judith Hamera (eds.), *The Cambridge Companion to American Travel Writing*. (Cambridge: University Press, 2009), particularly chapters 6 and 7.

[3] Frederick Marryat, "How to Write a Book of Travels," in *Olla Podrida*. Vol. III. London: (Longman, Orme, Brown, Green & Longmans, 1840), 529.

Marryat's satirical appreciation of travel writing is also echoed by twentieth-century critic Willard Thorp when he notes several pervasive conventions:

> The author must begin with the excitements of the ocean voyage itself and devote at least a portion of a chapter to the thrill, so long anticipated, of setting foot on foreign soil. From this point on he should mix architecture and scenery with comment on philanthropies, skillfully work in a little history cribbed from Murray's guides, taking care to add a touch of sentiment or eloquence when the occasion permitted. If the essay or book required a little padding, it was always possible to retell an old legend or slip in an account of dangers surmounted in crossing the Alps.[4]

Although both critics ridicule the genre, they also validate some of its main characteristics, namely the instructive and entertaining dimensions, almost always within a framework of respectability and truthfulness, or in other words the non-fictionality of these narratives. Notwithstanding, this is the Anglo-European travel narrative tradition whose object of observation is the foreigner, the Other.

However, the concept of travel, particularly referring to going abroad or engaging in foreign travel, did not often align with what one may classify as patriotic Americans. In general, throughout the nineteenth century, but particularly in the early national period until the Civil War, almost every major American writer made a comment ridiculing, criticizing, or at least questioning foreign travel, and almost every one of them wrote a book about travelling abroad. Perhaps the most famous example of this kind of contradictory impulse is Emerson's often quoted remark, from his 1841 essay "Self-Reliance," that "traveling is a fool's paradise,"[5] and then spent years traveling and even wrote *English Traits* (1856), a work which can be described as travel literature.

That remark is misleading because what Emerson was implying had more to do with the reasons why the Self/the individual traveled than with traveling itself.[6] The act of traveling, although enjoyable, often lacked self-

---

[4] Willard Thorp, "Pilgrim's Return," in *Literary History of the United States.* Volume 2. 3rd ed. Ed. Robert Spiller et al. (New York: Macmillan, 1969), 831.

[5] Ralph Waldo Emerson, "Self-Reliance," in *Essays* (Coradella Collegiate Bookshelf Editions, 2004), 64.

[6] See Isabel Oliveira Martins, "'Travelling is a fool's paradise': What we talk about when we talk about Emerson's views on travelling," in *Anglo Saxonica. Special Issue on Ralph Waldo Emerson*, Isabel Alves, Rochelle Johnson and Edgardo Medeiros da Silva (guest editors), Ser. III, N. 12, (Lisboa: ULICES 2016), 165-180.

reflection. Without introspection, there was a tendency to imitate, particularly when travel was pursued purely for recreation, as Emerson argues, "He who travels to be amused, or to acquire what he lacks, travels away from himself, and ages even in youth amidst old things."[7] If the traveler is the Artist then traveling to find "Beauty, convenience, grandeur of thought, and quaint expression"[8] may be misleading for the American artist. Ultimately, he has to look outside himself in order to create a new work, a new "house," in which the subject and the object will come together:

> … the American artist will study with hope and love the precise thing to be done by him, considering the climate, the soil, the length of the day, the wants of the people, the habit and form of the government, he will create a house in which all these will find themselves fitted, and taste and sentiment will be satisfied also.[9]

Thus, traveling, at least for the emerging American artist, would imply a search for the self, for an authentic experience which could help in the construct of identity both personal and quite soon national. Until late in the nineteenth century, traveling within the still developing United States was mostly seen as a means of spatial mobility, primarily physical, meaning movement between places or across space, and quite often that mobility implied other kinds of mobility – social, economic, even psychological and sexual.

Writing about traveling within the American territory required a distinctly American tradition, one that in the end combined elements of exploration and settlement of the territory with a quest for identity, which could ultimately result in a cultural analysis. By the end of the nineteenth century and beginning of the twentieth, some authors had already published their accounts of crisscrossing the country, not with a motorized vehicle, but still using the road even if rudimentary. Mark Twain's *Roughing It* (1872) is perhaps the most well-known work, one that he published after *Innocents Abroad* (1869), his account of traveling abroad to Europe and the Holy Land.

Still, it is in the twentieth century that "[t]he promise of mobility has taken shape in a century's worth of road films, novels, and nonfiction accounts that have popularized the road trip as a quintessential expression of

---

[7] Emerson, *op. cit.,* 63.
[8] Emerson, 64.
[9] Emerson, 64.

Americanness," as Ann Brigham argues.[10] The so-called American road narratives, a natural ramification of the travel narrative, aimed to "share a response to the idea of travel as a symbolic act, heavy with promises of new life, progress, and the thrill of escape."[11] The "idea of travel" as possibility and freedom leads to the examination of ideas of the individual in conflict with mass culture, and many road narratives analyze the role of nonconformity in understanding both the self and the country.

As many critics have remarked, notably Kris Lackey, Ronald Primeau, and Rowland A. Sherrill, American road narratives can be defined by two criteria: firstly, they are concerned with traveling the highways and back roads of America for self-discovery, cultural exploration, and critical inquiry. Secondly, road narratives deal with motor-powered transportation, whether by car, motorcycle, van, or truck. These two criteria are interrelated, since the rise of the automobile led understandably to the construction of interstate highways. Finally, road narratives can be non-fictional or fictional or both, such as Jack Kerouac's *On the Road* published in 1957 and considered one of the most representative of the genre.

When, in 1962, just some months prior to receiving the Nobel Prize for Literature, John Steinbeck published *Travels with Charley. In Search of America*,[12] the book was presented as a non-fictional account of Steinbeck's journey around the United States in a specially outfitted truck, Rocinante, accompanied by his French poodle, Charley, in the fall of 1960, from September 23 to December 5. The author's intentions are made clear in Part One of the book—which is divided into four parts—from the very first words. As a writer who had after all as his main subject America and Americans, he planned "to try to rediscover this monster land"[13]—meaning the United States of America—with which he wanted to refamiliarize himself after living for twenty-five years in New York:

> Thus I discovered that I did not know my own country. I, an American writer, writing about America, was working from memory, and the memory is at best a faulty, warpy reservoir. I had not heard the speech of America, smelled the grass and trees and sewage, seen its hills and water, its color and

---

[10] Ann Brigham, *American Road Narratives: Reimagining Mobility in Literature and Film*, (Charlottesville: University of Virginia Press, 2015), 3.
[11] Casey Blanton, *Travel Writing: The Self and the World*, (New York and London: Routledge, 2002), 18.
[12] John Steinbeck, *Travels with Charley. In Search of America*, (New York: Penguin Books, 1986).
[13] *Ibid.*, 6.

quality of light. I knew the changes only from books and newspapers. But more than this, I had not felt the country for twenty-five years. In short, I was writing of something I did not know about, and it seems to me that in a so-called writer this is criminal. My memories were distorted by twenty-five intervening years.[14]

He confesses that the years of separation from the America he had been writing about forced him to work from memory and the information offered by books and newspapers and this prevented him from "tell[ing] the small diagnostic truths which are the foundations of the larger truth."[15]

In addition to artistic motivation, Steinbeck portrays himself as a victim suffering from the "urge to be somewhere else" and the "virus of restlessness," those lifelong, incurable maladies taunted by "the road away from Here."[16] Moreover, he describes how, before leaving, he single-handedly saved his boat *Fayre Eleyne*, named after his third and present wife—Elaine Scott Steinbeck —during Hurricane Donna.[17]

The description of that successful task helps the author, who at the time was 58 and was having health problems,[18] to establish his manhood. In fact, at the beginning of Part Two he states: "My wife married a man; I saw no reason why she should inherit a baby. I knew that ten or twelve thousand miles driving a truck, alone and unattended, over every kind of road, would be hard work, but to me it represented the antidote for the poison of the professional sick man."[19]

Despite viewing his life as an artist and a man as inseparable, he still felt the need for isolation to confront his journey alone. However, this apparent solitude, as the reader learns throughout the text, included several interactions with his wife, friends, and stays at hotels and a family home in Texas. These experiences support the notion that his journey and subsequent narrative were in fact a meticulously crafted fictionalization of his quest, illustrating the disparity between perceived and actual reality. He refers to

---

[14] *Ibid., 5.*

[15] *Ibid.,* 6.

[16] *Ibid.,* 3.

[17] *Ibid.,* 14-17. The storm struck Long Island, New York, late on September 12 and rapidly weakened inland.

[18] John Steinbeck died in New York City on December 20, 1968, of heart disease and congestive heart failure. He was 66 and had been a lifelong smoker. An autopsy showed nearly complete occlusion of the main coronary arteries.

[19] *Ibid.,* 20.

this concept as "memory myth,"[20] an idealized vision of the past based largely on the recollections of his childhood in Salinas and personal experiences as a young writer in Monterey and other parts of Northern California. Despite journeying through America during a time of looming and irreparable transitions, the author fails to fully reclaim his constructed manhood or revive his creativity, resulting in criticisms of American culture and politics, as well as of himself. As he travels both on highways and back roads, he meets various Americans, leading him to compare what was with what is now. In his initial observations, Steinbeck laments the loss of local accents due to the standardized speech of radio and television, acknowledging that what he is mourning may not be worth saving but he still regrets its disappearance. He then goes on to criticize the loss of natural land in favor of industrial advancements, consumerism, associated waste, conformity, nuclear war paranoia, and political apathy. Steinbeck laments the "great hives of production" in towns such as Cleveland, Toledo, and Flint, as well as the "exploding production lines of the Middle West."[21]

He ridicules "The new American [who] finds his challenge and his love in traffic-choked streets, skies nested in smog, choking with the acids of industry, the screech of rubber and houses leashed in against one another while the townlets wither a time and die."[22] Another target for particular criticism is over-consumerism in urban spaces:

> ... cities are like badger holes, ringed with trash—all of them—surrounded by piles of wrecked and rusting automobiles, and almost smothered with rubbish. Everything we use comes in boxes, cartons, bins, the so-called packaging we love so much. The mountains of things we throw away are much greater than the things we use. In this, if in no other way, we can see the wild and reckless exuberance of our production, and waste seems to be the index.[23]

---

[20] *Ibid.,*207. In 2013, Bill Steigerwald published *Dogging Steinbeck: Discovering America and Exposing the Truth about 'Travels with Charley'*, the result of his own cross-country road trip following Steinbeck's itinerary in search of America, trying to prove that much of Steinbeck's book was a "literary fraud" (293), being not a non-fictional travelogue, but mostly fiction. Whether fictional or non-fictional, Steinbeck's work is mainly the result of a "real" journey he truly took and the result of his own way of working: "I also knew from thirty years of my profession that I cannot write hot on an event. It has to ferment. I must do what a friend calls "mule it over" for a time before it goes down." Steinbeck, 11.

[21] *Ibid.*, 108-109.

[22] *Ibid.*, 72.

[23] *Ibid.*, 26.

After spending time in various places, the author arrives in Salinas, California, where he had spent his formative years, while other writers were part of the "lost generation" in Paris. However, he soon realizes that the place of his origin has undergone significant change due to progress, while he had not evolved with it. During his stay in California, he lodges with his Republican sisters and engages in political discussions, which transform into a family "civil war," a reflection of the political and social upheaval of the era and the alterations in Steinbeck's personal convictions.[24] Additionally, a visit to a bar in Monterey, where old friends still reside, leads to a moment of realization for Steinbeck. As he tries to convince an old friend, Johnny Garcia, that he is no longer the person he once was, Johnny argues that Steinbeck's true home is not in New York, but rather in a life symbolized by the Monterey bar.[25] This confrontation of Steinbeck's present reality and Garcia's memory of him introduces the author to the environment of change, representing the present challenging the past and the irreconcilable distance between the two. The fleeting but lingering glimpse of California, a land Steinbeck refers to as "my country,"[26] leads him to conclude:

> My town had grown and changed and my friend along with it. Now returning, as changed to my friend as my town was to me, I distorted his picture, muddied his memory. When I went away I had died, and so became fixed and unchangeable. My return caused only confusion and uneasiness. Although they could not say it, my old friends wanted me gone so that I could take my proper place in the pattern of remembrance—and I wanted to go for the same reason. Tom Wolfe was right. You can't go home again because home has ceased to exist except in the mothballs of memory.[27]

Steinbeck further develops the metaphysical core of his journey by reflecting on his initial objective and what he has accomplished:

> It would be pleasant to be able to say of my travels with Charley, "I went out to find the truth about my country and I found it." And then it would be such a simple matter to set down my findings and lean back comfortably with a fine sense of having discovered truths and taught them to my readers. I wish it were that easy. But what I carried in my head and deeper in my perceptions was a barrel of worms…. External reality has a way of being not

---

[24] *Ibid.*, 198.
[25] *Ibid.*, 201-202.
[26] *Ibid.*, 189.
[27] *Ibid.*, 206.

so external after all. *This monster of a land, this mightiest of nations, this spawn of the future, turns out to be the macrocosm of microcosm me.* [28]

Steinbeck experiences a clash of emotions as he confronts his idealized vision of America and himself. He recognizes that change is an unavoidable reality, but at the same time, he feels resistant to it since it would force him to modify his own identity, something he is hesitant to do. Nonetheless, he tries to maintain an overall positive attitude towards America and its people, possibly due to his internal struggle:

> …these are my people and this my country. If I found matters to criticize and to deplore, they were tendencies equally present in myself. If I were to prepare one immaculately inspected generality it would be this: For all of our enormous geographic range, for all of our sectionalism, for all of our interwoven breeds drawn from every part of the ethnic world, we are a nation, a new breed. Americans are much more American than they are Northerners, Southerners, Westerners, or Easterners. And descendants of English, Irish, Italian, Jewish, German, Polish are essentially American. This is not patriotic whoop-de-do; it is carefully observed fact. California Chinese, Boston Irish, Wisconsin German, yes, and Alabama Negroes, have more in common than they have apart. And this is the more remarkable because it has happened so quickly…. It is astonishing that this has happened in less than two hundred years and most of it in the last fifty. The American identity is an exact and provable thing.[29]

However, relying solely on "exact and provable" things does not truly clarify anything, and American identity continues to exist as a collection of symbolic and stereotypical notions, indicating that the distinctiveness of America persists almost entirely in the realm of imagination and hopeful speculation. Meanwhile, the reader senses that as Steinbeck travels further east, he becomes increasingly aware of the deterioration of his own masculinity and creativity, which he had been attempting to regain.

Steinbeck's final observation relates to the matriculation of Negro students in a New Orleans school, the episode with the so-called "Cheerleaders/Cheerladies," a group of white mothers protesting against the integration of the public schools: "…in happy, almost innocent triumph when they were applauded. Theirs was the demented cruelty of egocentric children, and somehow this made their insensate beastliness much more heartbreaking. These were not mothers, not even women. They were crazy

---

[28] *Ibid.*, 209 (italics added).
[29] *Ibid.*, 210.

actors playing to a crazy audience."[30] Steinbeck exposes the climactic confrontation between progress towards civil rights in America and the resistance to change. His critical commentary on America's social ills, particularly the question of racial segregation in the South, is voiced not exactly through his words, but by giving the stage to several Americans he supposedly meets both before and afterwards. The attendant of the parking lot where he leaves Rocinante, the taxi driver who drives him to the scene, Monsieur Ci Gît, an elderly white man, an old Negro to whom he gives a ride, as well as another Southerner he meets at the motel and gives a ride, and finally a young Negro student, are the voices he uses to try to give an overall perspective on the subject.[31] Steinbeck's final comment is not exactly elucidatory and reveals his helplessness as well as his disillusion:

> With all the polls and opinion posts, with newspapers more opinion than news so that we no longer know one from the other, I want to be very clear about one thing. I have not intended to present, nor do I think I have presented, any kind of cross-section so that a reader can say, "He thinks he has presented a true picture of the South." I don't. I've only told what a few people said to me and what I saw. I don't know whether they were typical or whether any conclusion can be drawn. But I do know it is a troubled place and a people caught in a jam. And I know that the solution when it arrives will not be easy or simple. I feel with Monsieur Ci Gît that the end is not in question. It's the means—the dreadful uncertainty of the means.[32]

Following the episode with the Cheerleaders, and while on his way back home, Steinbeck continues to experience a sense of disenchantment with both his journey and his country. He becomes lost in downtown Manhattan, a situation that recurs several times. This could symbolize the bewildering state of America as he perceives it. It might also indicate Steinbeck's failure in his journey since he returns to New York, which he sees as the epicenter of a confusing dominant culture, thus somewhat confirming his status as a tourist in his own country. When he seeks assistance from a police officer, it appears that Steinbeck is acknowledging both the status quo in America and his life. The policeman represents law and order, and thus is a symbol of the existing conditions, and on the other hand by needing his help Steinbeck is also recognizing that he is not the man of the beginning of his travels who wanted to prove his manhood to his wife. The indifference and

---

[30] *Ibid.*, 258.
[31] *Ibid.*, 253-254 and 261-273.
[32] *Ibid.*, 273.

reluctance to social and political change he has encountered throughout his travels seems to have taken root in himself.

On one hand, the road, and the journey fail to provide Steinbeck with a real, sensory knowledge of what is truly America and American. Both his journey and his view of the America he traverses are layered with nostalgia. On the other hand, returning to the idea of the difference between a tourist and a traveler, in which the traveler would be the one who compared his own civilization with others, and rejected those elements he found not to his liking, one could argue that Steinbeck was a real traveler. Still, his civilization, or what he sees as his civilization, relies much more on the realm of fiction, of memory myth than on reality and therefore the conclusion is paradoxical: "But the more I inspected this American image, the less sure I became of what it is. It appeared to me increasingly paradoxical, and it has been my experience that when paradox crops up too often for comfort, it means that certain factors are missing in the equation."[33]

Steinbeck's work also allows, as well as other authors of road/travel narratives, to reflect on the fluidity between fact and fiction occurring in many of these narratives, as Frances Bartkowski argues:

> The demands placed upon the subject in situations of unfamiliarity and dislocation produce a scene in which the struggle for identity comes more clearly into view as both necessary and also mistaken . . . The subject, no matter how decentered, cannot not be a subject or it lapses into aphasia. We must speak, and once we do so we enact an enabling fiction of identity that makes social life possible.[34]

Whether fictional or non-fictional, Steinbeck's narrative is the result of his view of America or parts of it and ultimately he knew how subjective that would be:

> I feel that there are too many realities. What I set down here is true until someone else passes that way and rearranges the world in his own style. In literary criticism the critic has no choice but to make over the victim of his attention into something the size and shape of himself. And in this report I do not fool myself into thinking I am dealing with constants. For this reason I cannot commend this account as an America that you will find. So much there is to see, but our morning eyes describe a different world than do our

---

[33] *Ibid.*, 244.

[34] Frances Bartkowski, *Travelers, Immigrants, Inmates: Essays in Estrangement* (Minneapolis: University of Minnesota Press, 1995), xix-xx.

afternoon eyes, and surely our wearied evening eyes can report only a weary evening world.[35]

Thus, the America and the American road in this road narrative represent not a flight from opposition but a meeting place of clashing or contradictory elements, revealing even if inadvertently the complexity as well as the mythical allure of the road and making it America(n).

# Bibliography

Bartkowski, Frances. *Travelers, Immigrants, Inmates: Essays in Estrangement*. Minneapolis: University of Minnesota Press, 1995.

Bendixen, Alfred and Judith Hamera (eds.). *The Cambridge Companion to American Travel Writing*. Cambridge: Cambridge University Press, 2009.

Brigham, Anne. *American Road Narratives: Reimagining Mobility in Literature and Film*. Charlottesville: University of Virginia Press, 2015.

Bowles, Paul. *The Sheltering Sky*. 1949. London: Penguin Books, 2009.

Emerson, Ralph Waldo. "Self-Reliance." in *Essays*, 1841 Coradella Collegiate Bookshelf Editions, 2004.

Lackey, Kris. *RoadFrames: The American Highway Narrative*. Lincoln: University of Nebraska, 1997.

Marryat, Frederick. "How to Write a Book of Travels". *Olla Podrida*, 211-241. Vol. III. London: Longman, Orme, Brown, Green & Longmans, 1840.

Martins, Isabel Oliveira. "'Travelling is a fool's paradise': What we talk about when we talk about Emerson's views on travelling," In *Anglo Saxonica. Special Issue on Ralph Waldo Emerson*, 165-180. Ser. III, N. 12. Guest edited by Isabel Alves, Rochelle Johnson and Edgardo Medeiros da Silva. Lisboa: ULICES, 2016.

Mills, Katie. *The Road Story and the Rebel. Moving Through Film, Fiction, and Television*. Carbondale: Southern Illinois University Press, 2006.

Primeau, Ronald (ed.). *Critical Insights: American Road Literature*. New York: Grey House Publishing, Inc., 2013.

Sherrill, Rowland A. *Road-Book America. Contemporary Culture and the New Picaresque*. Urbana and Chicago: University of Illinois Press, 2000.

Spiller, Robert et al. *Literary History of the United States*. Volume 2. 3rd ed. New York: Macmillan, 1969.

---

[35] Steinbeck, 76-77.

Steigerwald, Bill. *Dogging Steinbeck: Discovering America and Exposing the Truth about 'Travels with Charley'*. Copyright Bill Steigerwald, 2013.

Steinbeck, John. *Travels with Charley. In Search of America*. 1962. Reissued. New York: Penguin Books, 1986.

Thorp, Willard. "Pilgrim's Return". In *Literary History of the United States*. 827-842. Volume 2. 3rd ed. Ed. Robert Spiller et al. New York: Macmillan, 1969.

Tuckerman, H.T. "Going Abroad". In *Putnam's Monthly Magazine of American Literature, Science and Art*. 530-538. Volume 1, Issue 5 May. New York: G. P. Putnam & Son, 1868.

# CHAPTER SIX

# THE BIRTH OF A ROAD.[1]
# THE *SOCIOPOÉTIQUE* OF MODERN
# INFRASTRUCTURE IN MICHEL MOUTOT'S
# NOVEL *ROUTE ONE* (2022)

## MELANIE SCHNEIDER

Thirty-three great roads lead out of Washington; as the Roman roads once led out of Capitol, they branch out into the circumference of the United States and trace a circulation of 25,747 miles. The posts were mounted on several of these roads. One takes the stagecoach to Ohio or Niagara, as in my day, one takes a guide or Indian interpreter. These means of transportation are twofold: lakes and rivers exist everywhere, linked together by canals, and one may travel along the land roads on rowboats and sails, water coaches, or steamers.

—François de Chateaubriand, *Mémoires d'Outre-tombe*[2]

---

[1] The title is inspired by Maylis de Kerangal's novel *Naissance d'un pont* (trad. *Birth of a Bridge*) (2010), telling the meticulous story of the construction of a highway bridge in an imaginary Californian city, and therefore dealing with another crucial element of infrastructure.

[2] Original quotation: "Trente–trois grandes routes sortent de Washington, comme autrefois les voies romaines partaient du Capitole ; elles aboutissent, en se ramifiant, à la circonférence des Etats–Unis, et tracent une circulation de 25,747 milles. Sur un grand nombre de ces routes, les postes sont montées. On prend la diligence pour l'Ohio ou pour Niagara, comme de mon temps on prenait un guide ou un interprète indien. Ces moyens de transport sont doubles : des lacs et des rivières existent partout, liés ensemble par des canaux ; on peut voyager le long des chemins de terre sur des chaloupes à rames et à voiles, ou sur des coches d'eau, ou sur des bateaux à vapeur", book 8, chapter 5, 525-26. *Mémoires d'outre-tombe* was published posthumously in two volumes in 1849 and 1850 and was started in 1809. The passage quoted here was originally written in 1821. Translation is author's own.

In 1789, François-René de Chateaubriand, a prominent figure in French literature, politics, historiography, and regarded as the father of French Romanticism, embarked on a voyage to America. Notably in the year 1822, approximately 33 years after his sojourn, Chateaubriand provided an account of his observations, specifically highlighting two remarkable infrastructural developments prevalent during that era: roads and water channels. According to German historian Drik van Laak, these two can be classified as physical and material infrastructure constituting the "stable [part], which is necessary to enable mobility and the exchange of people, goods, and ideas."[3] Therefore, the significance of infrastructure for humanity cannot be overestimated. This is especially true for roads that, to a greater extent than natural waterways,[4] experienced further development due to technical progress during the late 1800s and early 1900s. Only 90 years after Chateaubriand's description of the then still rudimentary and unpaved road network and around 60 years after his death in 1848, construction works began for one of America's epic *modern* roads, Route One. In accordance with Christoph Merki who distinguishes between premodern and modern transport, the second referring to mechanized transport based on (steam) engine and capital-intensive infrastructure, the adjective 'modern' in this sense refers to material and capital intensive infrastructure, for which construction machines and technological knowhow are required.[5] In light of these observations, it becomes apparent that men and women actively participate in the construction and implementation of an infrastructure, which, in turn, exerts a compelling influence on their "culture, [their] daily life, [their] consciousness, and [their] cultural technology."[6] The impact of infrastructure, including Route One specifically, extends beyond its physical construction. Its influence can be traced back to the conceptual stage. The fundamental concept behind the

---

[3] Van Laak, 13. Original quotation: "Infrastruktur könnte man definieren als alles Stabile, das notwendig ist, um Mobilität und einen Austausch von Menschen, Gütern und Ideen zu ermöglichen", translation is author's own.

[4] Jean Raspail's travelogue *En canot sur les chemins d'eau du Roi, une aventure en Amérique*, published in 2005, recounts the author's seven-month journey in 1949 in the company of three friends with whom he navigated the waterways of New France (Nouvelle-France) following the same route as Father Marquette, a Jesuit missionary who explored the Mississippi River in 1673. This travelogue provides a fascinating experience of America's water infrastructure.

[5] Van Laak, 10. This definition also coincides with the first use of the word *infrastructure* in French, which described the preliminary work needed to lay the railroad tracks (see Schwind/Obst 1972: 303).

[6] Van Laak, 9. Original quotation: "Kultur, unser Alltagsleben, unser Bewusstsein und unsere Kulturtechniken" (9), translation is author's own.

subsequent project, much like the earlier Pacific Railroad endeavor (1863-69)[7] primarily embodies a (socio-)political vision of a united, advanced, prosperous, and consequently powerful nation, while simultaneously projecting the desires and aspirations of the American people. Furthermore, the construction process itself – which took over two decades – shaped the imaginary around Route One and contributed to its fascination, attraction, and myth-building. This birth process – understood in both its real and figurative sense – and more precisely its literary representation depicted by the French author Michel Moutot in his novel *Route One* (2022), is at the center of this study. Methodically, our analysis follows the socio-poetical (*sociopoétique*) approach according to Alain Montandon, where literary texts are not considered as a simple reflection of a given social reality but function as a creative motor that shapes and motivates the social imaginary.[8] Regarding the numerous artistic works that in the past and present have thematized the American road, leading to its strong legendary mythification, this statement probably could not be truer.

After explaining the choice to discuss a French novel in a collective volume on anglophone literature and film and a short introduction to Moutot's work in general, this chapter examines the representation of Route One in the novel as a complex infrastructure project. This road venture, influenced by human will and executed through manpower, simultaneously impacts and shapes the lives of individuals directly engaged in its construction. Consequently, it highlights one of the main cultural attributes of infrastructure as discussed in this context.

The present volume focuses on the analysis of the imaginary of the road in anglophone literature and films. However, America – as we saw with Chateaubriand's citation at the beginning – became an object of interest to many French authors and thinkers of the 19th century who travelled to America, either physically (Chateaubriand, Alexis de Tocqueville), or vicariously through their fictional characters (Stendhal) [9] or through their intense occupation with some of its main political and literary figures

---

[7] The story about the construction of the first transcontinental railroad was told a few years ago in the American/Canadian Western television series *Hell on Wheels* (2011-2016), created and produced by Joe and Tony Gayton, illustrating the ongoing fascination regarding the great infrastructure projects of the modern era.

[8] Montandon, 2016

[9] E.g. Fabrice del Dongo and Lucien Leuwen from Stendhal's classics *La Chartreuse de Parme* (1839) and *Lucien Leuwen* (1894) travel to America (see Levergeois 2008).

(George Sand).[10] Later, in the 20th and 21st centuries, American road and car culture attracted authors from all over the world to reflect on their incomparable highways and enormous cars and their influence on the population and its practices. The *topos* of the American road (including its vehicles and sociotechnical installations such as the motel[11] and gas station[12]) inspired French authors and stimulated the production of travel narratives (Michel Butor's *Mobile* (1962)), socio-literary field studies (Bruce Bégout's *L'Éblouissement des bords de route* (2004)), and novels (Maylis de Kerangal's short story "Mustang" in *Canoës* (2021)). Therefore, Michel Moutot's *Route One* constitutes an additional part in the bigger picture of the French imaginary of the American road. Furthermore, the fascination of journalist and writer Moutot for America is reflected in his entire literary production: *Ciel d'acier* (2015) uses the example of the collapse of the Twin Towers of the World Trade Center to negotiate the history of America's steel monuments. More importantly, the history of the workers who created those towers, *Séquoias* (2018) tells the story of three brothers from a family of whalers who follow the call of gold from Nantucket to California in the mid-19th century, while *L'America* (2020) focuses on the wave of immigration from Italy to America as a result of the machinations of the mafia at the beginning of the 20th century. Inspired to tell the story of America through its major events and myths, it does not seem surprising that Moutot continues his vision by taking on the story of one of America's main roads.

As mentioned above, the novel illustrates the collective manpower and willpower needed to propel the advancement of civilization. It does so by creating a durable infrastructure that not only initiates but also is at the heart of the technical, ecological, political, and societal progress of the past century, encompassing both positive and negative outcomes. In other words, Moutot deviates from portraying the road as a metaphor for an individual's

---

[10] George Sand was not only fascinated by Benjamin Franklin but also wrote critical articles about Harriet Beecher-Stowe and Fenimore Cooper (see Schapira, 2011).

[11] See Elsa Court's contribution "'Stationary Trivialities': Contrasting Representations of the American Motel in Vladimir Nabokov and Jack Kerouac" in Aguiar, Marian Charlotte Mathieson, and Lynne Pearce, eds., *Mobilities, Literature, Culture*, (Cham: Palgrave Macmillan 2019), 65-86 where she compares the representation of the motel in two iconic novels of the road genre.

[12] See the article by Catherine Morgan-Proux, "Une sociopoétique des stations-service", *Sociopoétiques* [En ligne], 7, 2022, DOI : https://dx.doi.org/10.52497/sociopoetiques.1567 where she gives a first overview of the imaginary of the gas station in advertising, art and literature by drawing on French and English references.

life experiences and the accompanying perceptions and sensations, a convention notable in works like Jack Kerouac's *On the Road* (1957) in the coded road genre of literature and film. Instead, Moutot takes a step back, guiding his readers through the birth process of Route One. By doing so, Moutot does not limit himself to the technical details but confronts us with a kaleidoscope of narratives that emerge around the planning and construction of Route One as a piece of crucial infrastructure, and therefore gives us an insight into its historical, social, and political context linked to its myth-building. The novel's plot follows the young and promising engineer Wilbur Tremblay who, after working on the famous Hoover Dam, which marked the tremendous growth of Las Vegas, was given the task of building the last section of Route One, linking Canada to Mexico along the Pacific Ocean. Wilbur's antagonist in the novel is Hyrum Rock, a Mormon settler who came to the wild lands of California to continue with his constantly scrutinized polygamous lifestyle, opposing modern ideas of family life, and preferring to live on his ranch as if he were in the mid-19th century. The events in the novel are presented in a non-chronological manner, with chapters spanning the period between 1847, when Hyrum Rock's father arrived in California, and 1936, the year when Route One was completed. The final section of the novel specifically takes place between 1930 and 1936. Although Moutot's novel may be less convincing in terms of its aesthetics, language, and style – focusing therefore more on the "socio" than the "poetical" –, it succeeds in depicting the complex sociohistorical circumstances surrounding the birth of Route One, including the various perceptions of the project by different groups, making the novel interesting for an analysis of the road as if it were the main protagonist.

Two aspects of literary representation regarding Route One will be explored: on the one hand, the concrete construction of Route One as a metaphorically charged victory of humans over nature, and on the other hand, the repercussions the planned piece of modern infrastructure exerted on individual social groups. Working through these aspects will help us to better understand the imaginary of the American road in general and Route One in particular.

As indicated above, Wilbur embodies technological progress in the novel, while Rock can be seen as a personification of California's natural landscape. The nature/technology dichotomy is represented through the construction of Route One right at the beginning:

He hears the machine before seeing it. The hoarse breath of a beast of iron and coal, every three seconds. Track creation, mechanical grunts, rock cracking, and wisps of smoke and dust above the canyon. The echo of the bulldozer mingled with the rumor of the Pacific, covering it at times. So, it was true. These damned workers are no longer armed with shovels, picks, or wheelbarrows. The metal monster that he had seen disembark from a ship at Anderson Landing and climb toward the construction site, like a giant insect crushing everything in its path, went into action. Steam shovel.[13]

The novel begins with the impression of Rock, who sees the road as a violation of nature and, therefore, of the ancient world to which he feels a strong sense of belonging. At the same time, his description refers to the new construction technologies and marks the beginning of the modern era where humans can actively shape their environment and where technology enables them to overcome their inherent natural limitations. The description therefore marks the development of man towards Freud's depicted "prothetic God" in his famous *Civilization and Its Discontents* of 1930, published six years before the finalization of the part of Route One along the Pacific Ocean coastline. In its constitution, the new machinery offers new sensory experiences; notably, Rock's hearing and vision must be adjusted to this spectacle. The image in the quotation cited at the beginning to describe the modern tools and their effect on the construction site remind us of Émile Zola's description of the train as "human beast" (*bête humaine*) and describe the machine as an unnatural and technological threatening creature that devours everything in its way in the landscape: "Menace of iron and fire, symbol of the new century, mechanical barbarian, it [the shovel] violates the lost paradise of the wild coast"[14] (RO 11). Throughout the novel, Rock tries to stop the ongoing work on Route One. However, the following chapter illustrates the advantages of modern infrastructure by describing the struggles of a rudimentary infrastructure project dated to

---

[13] (*Route One* :11) Original quotation: "Il entend la machine avant de la voir. Le souffle rauque d'une bête de fer et de charbon, toutes les trois secondes. Grincements de chenilles, grognements mécaniques, craquements de roches, volutes de fumée et de poussière au-dessus du canyon. L'écho du bulldozer se mêle à la rumeur du Pacifique, la couvre par moments. C'était donc vrai. Ces maudits ouvriers ne sont plus armés que de pelles, de pioches et de brouettes. Le monstre de métal qu'il a vu débarquer d'un navire à Anderson Landing et monter vers le chantier, comme un insecte géant écrasant tout sur son passage, est entrée en action. Une pelle à vapeur," translation is author's own. References to the novel are followed by the abbreviation RO in the text.
[14] Original quotation: "Menace de fer et de feu, symbole du siècle nouveau, barbare mécanique, elle (la pelle) viole le paradis perdu de la côte sauvage." Translation is author's own.

1915 – this is 20 years before Rock's observation mentioned above – that constantly needs to be rebuilt because of its inadequate construction and its exposure to a hostile environment:

> Here in St. Clouds, a logging town founded in a deep valley of the Maine River by Quebec lumberjacks in the mid-19th century, the carpenters knew that before they could begin their summer work, they had to rebuild the log bridges that had fallen victim to the ice breakup and its floods. Not all of them were washed away, but they had to be checked and consolidated at best, and at worst, dismantled and rebuilt with larger logs, knowing that everything would certainly have to be redone the following year[15] (RO 15).

This scene describes the harsh and time-consuming process, contingent upon weather conditions and the pre-industrial reality of human shaping of the natural world to guarantee the coexistence and cohabitation that is in its most basic composition related to infrastructure. The rudimentary character of the wood bridges in question as fugitive infrastructure is also reinforced by the following comparison to modern equipment applied during the construction of Road One, which was also the cause of criticism of Hyrum Rock earlier in the text: "Here, there is no metal or reinforced concrete, no asphalt and paint, and no signage, like on the coast. In central Maine, the trails are dirt, rustic communities, and log structures"[16] (RO 15). One of the bridges described here connects the orphanage where Wilbur lived until his adoption. Due to damage, the orphanage is cut off from its source of supplies, and when Wilbur observes the reconstruction works of the bridge, he discovers his fascination with infrastructure and decides that one day he will be an engineer. Wilbur's early experience illustrates the idea and function of infrastructure as a vital network for society that appears several times throughout the novel in discussions about Route One (see RO 236, 242).

---

[15] Original quotation: "Ici à St Clouds, bourgade forestière fondée dans une vallée encaissée du Maine par des bûcherons québécois au milieu du XIXe siècle, les charpentiers savent qu'avant d'attaquer les chantiers estivaux ils doivent au printemps reconstruire les ponts de rondins victimes de la débâcle et de ses crues. Tous ne sont pas emportés, mais ils doivent être au mieux vérifiés et consolidé, au pire démontés et rebâtis avec des troncs plus gros, en sachant que tout sera certainement à refaire l'année suivante." Translation is author's own.

[16] Original quotation: "Ici, pas de métal ou de béton armé, pas d'asphalte et de peinture, de panneaux de signalisation, comme sur les routes de la côte. Dans le centre du Maine, les pistes sont en terre, les communautés rustiques et les structures en rondins." Translation is author's own.

The latter presents a particular challenge in that, during the westward development, it is the "*route du bout du monde*," which, as the novel's bookcover of the Seuil edition illustrates, runs along the cliffs on the Pacific Ocean and whose construction therefore involves a certain amount of risk for engineers and workers (see RO 155-157). Simultaneously, the effort required contributes to a heightened sense of victory over nature. Despite the natural conditions and Rock's attempts at sabotage, the expansion of Route One moves forward. The showdown between Wilbur and Rock seals the victory of modern technology over the old natural supremacy. Wilbur falls in love with Rock's eldest daughter, who wants to flee her Mormon life and be together with Wilbur. When Rock discovers the betrayal of his daughter, he attacks Amelia and Wilbur, and Rock is killed by Amelia's mother. Wilbur needs to get rid of Rock's corpse, deciding to embed it in the construction of Route One:

> Twenty minutes later, he arrives at the site where a reinforced concrete retaining wall is to be poured the next day. The formwork is in place. The structure, which supports the road at a bend on the road below Route One, is three meters high at the base and two meters high at the top. In the glow of the headlights, the engineer unloads his cargo and tips it between the planks. The rancher's body falls to the bottom with a thud followed by his rifle. Shovels of earth made him disappear from the sight of the masons who, the next morning, will not understand why the big boss of the construction site had come to supervise the pouring of concrete. At 11 o'clock, Hyrum Rock's corpse is swallowed up forever by forty-six tons of sand, gravel, and cement[17] (RO 302-303).

This act symbolizes on the one hand the incorporation of nature by technological progress, and on the other hand, the palimpsest character of the modern road, referring to its genesis. At the end of Moutot's novel the inauguration of Route One is finalized through the symbolic act of rolling the last remaining stone of the road into the ocean: "After the majorettes and a parade of forest rangers on horseback, a bulldozer approaches in slow

---

[17] Original quotation: "Vingt minutes plus tard, il arrive à l'emplacement où, le lendemain, un mur de soutènement en béton armé doit être coulé. Les coffrages sont en place. L'ouvrage, qui soutient la chaussée dans un virage en contrebas de la route One, fait trois mètres à sa base, deux à son sommet. À la lueur des phares, l'ingénieur décharge sa cargaison et la fait basculer entre les planches. Le corps du rancher tombe au fond avec un bruit sourd, suivi de son fusil. Des pelletées de terre le font disparaître à la vue des maçons qui, le lendemain matin, ne comprendront pas pourquoi le big boss du chantier est venu superviser la coulée du béton. À onze heures, le cadavre de Hyrum Rock est englouti à jamais sous quarante-six tonnes de sable, de gravier et de ciment." Translation is author's own.

motion and, to cheers, pushes the boulder into the void, bouncing from rock
to rock and plunging into the ocean. The road is officially open"[18] (OR,
314). Ultimately, civilization prevails over nature. This rough land by the
cliffs that presented a real challenge to Wilbur Tremblay and the workers,
is finally overcome by human willpower and the dream of a connected
country, linking therefore the image of the road not only to human progress
but also awarding it an identity-forming function.

Although the novel ends with the completion of Route One and therefore
no driving scene is depicted in the text, the future of Route One and its
sociotechnical potential is made clear by Wilbur's ride on a motorbike from
Maine to Chicago to the Route One construction site on the Atlantic Coast,
which he relates to the owner of the Rocky Mountains Hotel during his stay:

> Will tells of beautiful sunsets and dawns of dogs biting his boots, of four flat
> tires, of the providential bridge in Indiana that sheltered him from a
> hailstorm, of rifle shots fired into the air by a farmer to dissuade him from
> entering his yard; the hospitality of a recent Russian immigrant family near
> Omaha who barely spoke English but refused to let him sleep in the barn and
> offered him the bed of the eldest of their six children, the arrest by an Ohio
> State Police motorcyclist on a Harley Davidson who had nothing against him
> but wanted to compare the two. He wanted to compare the merits of their
> machines (...)[19] (RO 241).

The description continues in a similar style, taking up almost an entire page
in the novel. It refers to Moutot's ambition to present America's main roads
as the social lifelines of the country, thus showing not only the technical
development of infrastructure as man's effect on nature as discussed above
but also its impact on the American population. On the one hand, the

---

[18] Original quotation: "Après les majorettes et une parade de gardes forestiers à
cheval, un bulldozer approche au ralenti et, sous les bravos, pousse dans le vide le
bloc de pierre qui rebondit de rocher en rocher et plonge dans l'océan. La route est
officiellement ouverte." Translation is author's own.

[19] Original quotation: "Will raconte les couchers de soleil et les aubes magnifiques,
les chiens mordant ses bottes, ses quatre crevaisons, le pont providentiel qui dans
l'Indiana l'a abrité d'un orage de grêle, les coups de fusil tirés en l'air par un fermier
pour le dissuader d'entrer dans sa cour, l'hospitalité d'une famille d'immigrants
russes de fraîche date, près d'Omaha, qui parlaient à peine l'anglais mais ont refusé
qu'il dorme dans la grange et lu ont offert le lit de l'aîné de leurs six enfants,
l'arrestation par un motard de la police de l'état de l'Ohio en Harley Davidson, qui
n'avait rien à lui reprocher mais voulait comparer les mérites de leurs machines
(…)." Translation is author's own.

description makes it clear that the road knows no social hierarchy;[20] on the other hand, it reinforces Moutot's intention to depict the influence of Route One as infrastructure, not on the individual, but on American society as a whole.

All the characters and groups that appear in the novel – be they the convicts brought in to work at Big Sur, the workers, Hyrum Rock's family and their neighbors, or Wilbur – see their fates affected by the construction of Route One and by the promise associated with it. In particular, the workers who were hired on the construction site of Route One perceive the road as an escape from the economic crisis: "the workers unemployed since the beginning of the crisis of '29 and just hired on the site see it as the end of their nightmare, a return to work, the satisfaction of holding a tool"[21] (RO 40). Of course, workers were also exploited and faced harsh working conditions. Nevertheless, in their minds, the road gave them hope and enabled them to provide for their needs and those of their families.

Workers are among those whose lives are influenced by the concrete construction process. Amelia and Rock's neighbors, the Pfeiffers, on the other hand, project their hopes and imaginations onto the unfinished road. Amelia hopes to escape the constraints of traditional Mormon culture and participate in the social life of the modern world. Her neighbors, who unlike Rock's, have been trying to open themselves up to the world for a long time by welcoming regular tourists to their land, hope that the connection will bring them even more visitors and thus, above all, an economic improvement:

> The Pfeiffer Resort offers horseback riding, barbecuing, hunting, fishing, and hiking in the spectacular scenery and pristine nature of Big Sur to city dwellers from Monterey, and sometimes San Francisco. For the Pfeiffers, the arrival of the road was a blessing and offered unhoped opportunities for expansion[22] (RO 245).

---

[20] This conception of the street as a community-building installation where people of all backgrounds and classes can meet is central to the constitution of the road genre (see Laderman 2002, Virant 2019).

[21] Original quotation: "les ouvriers au chômage depuis le début de la crise de 29 et tout juste embauchés sur le chantier y voient la fin de leur cauchemar, un retour au travail, la satisfaction d'empoigner un outil." Translation is author's own.

[22] Original quotation: "Le Pfeiffer Resort propose aux citadins venus de Monterey et parfois de San Francisco balades à cheval, barbecues, chasse, pêche et promenades dans les paysages spectaculaires et la nature vierge de Big Sur. Pour les Pfeiffer, l'arrivée de la route est une bénédiction et offre des perspectives d'expansion inespérées." Translation is author's own.

Both Amelia and the Pfeiffer family project their aspirations and desires for what they envision as a better life. Moutot manages here to trace the effect that Route One exerts in its nature as a sociotechnical installation even before its actual commissioning, showing that the imaginary of the modern road takes form, and so can be explored and analyzed, long before the official inauguration date.

This chapter aimed to provide a French perspective on the imaginary of the American road through an analysis of Michel Moutot's novel *Route One*. Of particular interest in Moutot's work was the focus on the construction of the road and the future promises and aspirations ignited by the concrete, tangible process. The goal was to highlight the cultural imaginary of Route One and to show that its significance is not limited to the future functions of the facility, but rather is already nurtured during the planning stage and throughout the physical creation process. In the case of Moutot's novel, the imaginary feeds on the concrete construction of the modern road as indispensable infrastructure and its associated metaphorically charged victory of technological progress over nature, personified in the novel by the characters Hyrum Rock and Wilbur Tremblay. Furthermore, the cultural representation of the road is fueled by projections of the longings and desires of various groups of actors waiting for the road to be *birthed*.

## Bibliography

Court, Elsa. "'Stationary Trivialities': Contrasting Representations of the American Motel in Vladimir Nabokov and Jack Kerouac" In Aguiar, Marian, Charlotte Mathieson, and Lynne Pearce, eds. *Mobilities, Literature, Culture.* Cham: Palgrave Macmillan (2019): 65-86.

De Chateaubriand, François. *Mémoires d'Outre-tombe.* Tome 1, Livres I à XII. Paris: Garnier, 1989.

Laderman, David. *Driving Vision. Exploring the Road Movie.* Texas: University of Texas Press, 2002.

Levergeois, Bertrand. "Stendhal contre l'Amérique", *Humanisme* 281 (2008/2) : 113-115. DOI: 10.3917/huma.281.0113.

Merki, Christoph. *Verkehrsgeschichte und Mobilität.* Stuttgart: Ulmer UTB, 2008.

Montandon, Alain. "Sociopoétique", *Sociopoétiques* 1 (2016). DOI: 10.52497/sociopoetiques.640.

Morgan-Proux, Catherine. "Une sociopoétique des stations-service". *Sociopoétiques* 7, (2022). DOI: https://dx.doi.org/10.52497/sociopoetiques.1567.

Moutot, Michel. *Route One*. Paris : Seuil, 2022.

Schapira, Marie-Claude. "George Sand et l'Amérique." In Bara, Olivier, and Christine Planté, eds. *George Sand critique: Une autorité paradoxale*. Saint-Étienne: Presses universitaires de Saint-Étienne (2011). DOI:
https://doi.org/10.4000/books.puse.2469.

Schwind, Martin, and Erich Obst, *Allgemeine Staatengeographie*. Berlin: de Gruyter, 1972.

Van Laak, Dirk. *Alles im Fluss. Die Lebensadern unserer Gesellschaft – Geschichte unnd Zukunft der Infrastruktur*. Frankfurt am Main: Fischer (2018).

Virant, Špela. "Road Novel. Zur gattungstheoretischen Begriffsbestimmung." *Zeitschrift für Literaturwissenschaft und Linguistik* 49 (2019): 633 - 651.

CHAPTER SEVEN

THE ROAD ACCORDING
TO A YOUNG TEENAGER:
THE EXAMPLE OF GRACE,
A NOVEL BY PAUL LYNCH

LEISHA ASHDOWN-LECOINTRE

The road in all its forms, both literal and figurative, criss-crosses *Grace*, a novel by Paul Lynch published by Oneworld in 2017, then translated into French by Marina Boraso and published by Albin Michel in 2019. It played a strong social role during the Great Famine in Ireland, from 1845-1849, as it acted as a gathering space for those looking desperately for food. Approximately one sixth of the population was decimated by this tragic event - from 8.4 million inhabitants at the beginning of the famine, the population dropped to 6.6 million in 1851.[1] Even if the author does not appreciate the term "historical novel" in relation to *Grace*, the events recounted and experienced, seemingly first-hand, make the misery and horror of this period painfully real. Forced to leave her home at age fourteen, Grace is propelled unwillingly into the adult world. This *bildungsroman* follows the character from a young teenager until the age of nineteen. In her company, the reader discovers the ever-present dangers on the road, full of pitfalls, as well as the omnipresence of death. The constant challenges of the famine and her resilience despite countless obstacles make Grace a finely woven and nuanced character.

Grace, the novel's namesake, is thrust into a fight for her own survival when cast out by her mother from their house in Northern Ireland. She is told to take the road towards the South West in search of work and food. Grace covers a distance of approximately 800 km on foot as she travels through

---

[1] https://www.britannica.com/event/Great-Famine-Irish-history, [consulted 6 February 2020].

the novel. This imposed exile is ostensibly for two reasons: the first being
that Grace's mother Sarah wants her daughter, the eldest of four children,
with another on the way, to provide at least in part for the family's needs.
However, the second and more pressing reason is that she wants to protect
Grace from her partner's sexual advances. This tall prepubescent girl must
dress as a boy in order to better her chances of finding work. Sarah advises
her to impersonate her brother Colly, but Grace ends up being called Tim,
her cousin's name, by one of her employers. Her first job as a cattle-driver
takes her along a somewhat difficult path, dressed in her deceased father's
clothes. These initial experiences of the road lead us to question its role in
this coming-of-age novel. High road, low road, walkway, dead end road,
track, trail, path, the unrelenting presence of an itinerary keeps both Grace
and the reader in constant motion. How does the painful experience of being
forced out of home and onto the road affect the character's development?
Firstly, we will investigate the road from a literal standpoint, according to
Grace's experiences on the road, before considering her metaphorical
journey towards an affirmed identity. In a final part, we will question
Grace's spiritual journey and the transcending power of the sacred,
according to the author.

From her first meeting with the physical road which leads her across a large
portion of Ireland, Grace comes to know and identify with it like an old
friend. As a cattle-driver she must guide the cattle along the right path,
thereby showing them the way to food and shelter. During this work
assignment, Grace's team gets lost, disoriented by wetlands which hide and
deform the countryside. The winter snow cover hides the road at the moment
when Grace tries to save her workmate suffering from fever, having lost
both his money and clothes during a road-side assault. Literally feeling their
way along the road, Grace and her work companion, John Bart, take refuge
where they can, in abandoned or rundown farm houses on the roadside, and
sometimes hide in the forests or behind hills. The search for food, shelter or
basic protection from the attacks of other famine sufferers, means that
remaining on track is literally and metaphorically a question of survival. In
fact, John Bart ends up succumbing to infection, and Grace continues her
journey once again alone.

Being physically lost on the road is a recurring experience for Grace. As she
leads a hand-to-mouth existence, her priority is to find paid work allowing
her to eat enough to survive. Dressed as a young man, she locates a public
worksite where she is paid 7 pence per day, the daily rate for an underage

worker. Called the "Harrow,"[2] this worksite recalls the programme of public works instigated by the British government during the Great Famine. It allowed the suffering population to earn the minimum wage and thus to eat one meal per day. The harrow evokes an agricultural implement; it is indeed a trope symbolising the reduction of the workers to the state of human machines. Their physical state is checked regularly and those showing signs of fatigue or weight loss struggle to hide their physical state under penalty of losing their job. The author, either on purpose or by accident later calls the same worksite the "Hollow"[3]: by sheer brute strength, the workers hollow out the physical road, in a state of physical emptiness as their bodies yearn for food. Nevertheless, their labour seems to yield little result; according to the narrator, the road being constructed by at least one hundred men and women leads nowhere: "Foot by foot this going-nowhere road deepens through the bog, gathering new workers into its expression of noise and mud and tree bones."[4] Elsewhere in his work, Paul Lynch expresses a political point of view on what he considers the incapacity of the Irish to construct roads. In his first novel, *Red Sky in Morning*, he writes:

> The Danes and the Normans they built your roads too. The Irish never even founded a road. Imagine that. Thousands of years trudging in the rain and the mud, back and forth, to and fro; in our bare feet, up to your knees in cow shit. It must have been slow going that on your primitive paths. And nobody not once thought of making a road. You had to be helped with that too, didn't you?[5]

Roads leading nowhere, or badly constructed roads, the difficulty of finding your way as a traveller seems insurmountable.

On the public worksite, Grace bends under the weight of her wheelbarrow and menstrual pains: her first period publicly betrays her disguise and forces her to leave her employ under penalty of sexual aggression from some male workmates. This humiliating experience marks a turning point in her life journey: without a confidante in the absence of her mother, Grace digs deep into her memory, remembering different allusions about this unexplained and strange loss of blood. Persuaded that she may die from it, she has a sleepless night of mind travel looking for pathways delving into a fuller knowledge of her new self. From this point onwards, her femininity will take over, making her even more desperate in a perilous world in a state of

---

[2] Paul Lynch, *Grace*, (London: One World, 2017), 151.
[3] *Ibid*, 160.
[4] *Ibid*.
[5] Paul Lynch, *Red Sky in Morning*, (London: Quercus, 2013), 39-40.

total decomposition. Nevertheless, while her true identity catches up with her, Grace begins a new stage in her life by becoming conscious of her femininity. Her own story is written with blood on the road. A ghost met on the road explains the menstrual cycle to Grace. By referring to the concepts of signified (meaning) and signifier (graphemes) invented by Ferdinand de Saussure, the reader can better understand the relationship Grace perceives between her new-found femininity and death through blood loss. Without doubt, her survival depends on her ability to hide her womanly body and its telltale signs. The signifier, that is the menstrual blood, weakens Grace's mental state because the meaning of this blood, that is the mental representation she has of it, is one of a slow and uncontrollable agony leading to death, which comes back regularly to haunt her. In the same way, the ghost of the victim of a holdup staged by Grace and her companions, as well as other ghosts in the novel, weave their threatening way back and forth into her consciousness. Let us recall that Grace is sent out onto the road at the Samhain, the title of the first chapter of the novel, evoking the Irish celebration of the Day of the Dead or the American Halloween when it was believed that the ghosts of dead ones would return to visit their family. It was also a time of bonfires and dressing up, a custom descended from pagan beliefs. Shocked to be confronted by one of her victims, Grace realises that death is inescapable:

> Her body moves involuntary along the shepherd path, kicks at loosened scree, her mind meeting images unbidden of woman and man and child and blood mingled into a family of death and this is what happens, she thinks, you get what you ask for. It is one thing for the living to track you down to your hillside hideout but the dead always know where you are.[6]

Further along in the novel, the return of her periods after an interruption of a year caused by malnutrition, will spark a public ceremony: the rag soiled by menstrual blood is waved in front of the captive audience as being a miraculous sign of this nearly dead woman's recovery. Grace's femininity is difficult to hide; each time it manifests itself, Grace is followed by a man intending to sexually assault her.

When Grace takes up her journey once again, she tries to flee the lustful looks of men, a real danger for a young woman alone in the open. Continuing to hide her feminine forms is of the utmost importance. Together with a workmate who has a deformed right arm and his long-time friend, Grace forms a trio of bandits crisscrossing the roads and robbing the rich, like Robin Hood, however the gains are not shared beyond the small group.

---

[6] Grace, *op.cit.,* 227.

Initiated into the use of knives, Grace learns to defend herself. Moreover, the trio steals shotguns from a group of policemen on the road before shooting and killing a young couple, leaving their baby an orphan. Once again recognised as being a woman, Grace tries all the harder to show no pity but the crime provokes nothing more than remorse when faced with the ghost of the young married woman killed during the attack. Grace believes she is being stalked not only by the living, but also the dead. However, the author, in his description of this failed armed holdup, underlines the role of one of Grace's accomplices who lights a fire along the roadside to frighten the victims of the attack. The bandit climbs up on the roof of the horse-drawn cab where he assumes a devil's appearance, because of the flames, and the scene is transformed into an apocalyptic scene from Dante. As a symbol of death, he becomes a winged monster. During an earlier armed holdup, the same bandit had stolen stag horns from the house of a member of the Public Works committee. He uses them as a disguise, the horns bearing out his evil and monstrous nature. With the survival of the fittest, death seems to sweep everything aside in its path. Reduced to transgressing the law, Grace discovers a level of existence between life and death. With her two accomplices, she seems to side with death. Realising to her horror that she is capable of killing someone, or at least of aiding and abetting a murder, she discovers a level of existence so dehumanising that it could morally annihilate her.

The episode of the armed holdup is an extension of the theme of survival, already shown on the worksite where she tries to earn her living through honest hard labour. When her identity is discovered, she can no longer continue in the job and thus loses her ability to live decently. Paul Lynch points to the correlation between Grace on the public worksite and the dehumanisation of society:

> They [the public works] are also symptomatic of an attitude towards the working poor, the displaced, the victims of society. It speaks of a dehumanisation that is all too common, in the past, and today. If my writing seeks out these contrasts, between how society sees certain individuals as non-individuals, while at the same time, I allow the reader to fully inhabit my characters, it is because I am interested in the idea of dignity, that dignity can never be conferred by the individual upon themselves. It is something that can be given only by society, or by the act of an artist as intermediary, making a claim on behalf of an individual to society. I believe this act of rehabilitation is an essential task for the author.[7]

---

[7] Quoted from a personal email of 9 December 2019 signed by Paul Lynch.

In effect the Public Works scheme allowed the British government to pay a token salary to workers, for very laborious work: they were effectively treated as workhorses labouring in menial activity. We can thereby appreciate a timeless aspect of this novel: drawing upon the Irish famine, the post-apocalyptic vision in Grace resonates today with the desperate situation of countless refugees and immigrants buffeted by a society pushed to its extremes by the sheer size of the humanitarian crisis. A poignant image of the debasement of humankind in the novel is even more striking: during their escape after the failed holdup, Grace and her accomplices jump into a cooper's cab. As the road goes dangerously down towards a precipice the cab falls into a ditch. Stunned by their fall, they see the corpse of a young man tied to the wheel of a cart. Around his neck they see a sign indicating "Thief."[8] Grace becomes mute in the face of such a barbaric act: "She cannot speak, can only think of the awfulness of such an act, who would tie a dead boy to a cart wheel like that?"[9] The author invites the reader to reflect on the premises of such a society and on the correlations with our own.

A growing mutism takes Grace over little by little, underlining the relationship between the physical and moral states in the novel. Just as the violence present in 1840s Ireland leaves Grace voiceless, famine victims gradually lose their ability to speak as they die of hunger. As the senses succumb to hunger, the outside world starts fading away. The cacophony of the road begins to diminish at the moment Grace has her coat stolen and faces up to winter with no real shelter. Forced towards the towns, Grace tries to feed herself by begging in the streets but is confronted with the apathy of passersby. The town streets, often described as triangles or diamonds, fascinate Grace, the country bumpkin, because of their sheer size. Here is the home of the rich who possess horse-drawn carriages and live there, the roads multiply into mazes of streets. In contrast, the country road is clearly visible and starkly dressed; it leads to more emptiness, that of the countryside and that of the famine victims whose muffled voices become ever more quiet as fatigue takes over. Grace's train of thoughts as she begs in the city streets challenge the reader to question the foundation of a society of the voiced and the voiceless:

---

[8] *Grace, op.cit.*, 250.
[9] *Ibid.*

> She thinks, there is a gap widening between the luckless and the lucked. [...]
> It is the lucked who prise open the road's silence. Carriages thunder the road
> as if nothing were the matter. People passing by on their way to the city or
> for ship's passage, some of them dressed in their best clothes as if traveling
> to mass or a fair. Their belongings heaped and roped down. She wants to
> shout, the city is a trick -- you think you can hide on its streets and escape
> this wintering but the city will eat you up. At least in the country the
> wintering sits on the road plain as daylight and you know where you are at.[10]

Deliverance does not exist, especially for those dying of hunger, voiceless
and listless, on the side of the road as Grace's companion John Bart
expresses: "But who is going to deliver them? Not God and not the Crown
and not anybody in this country."[11]

Left to fend for herself, Grace begins the slow path to death; as a final resort
she eats tree bark, becomes delirious and feverish, and is on the verge of
dying. Picked up by sacristans at a ditch on the roadside, her inert body is
then transported to a mass grave. In a novel where each page is haunted by
death, whether in the face of a skeletal child dying from starvation or in the
sick whose slow and painful death seems interminable, Grace's passing
appears inevitable. Yet she is saved thanks to the intervention of a religious
fanatic. Called "father" by a good number of women converts who worship
him like God, this character personifies a twisted and evil religiousness. A
strong narrative thread runs through this novel with its evocative title,
"Grace"[12], and yet the portrayal of religion rhymes more with artifice,
trickery and physical suffering than with salvation.  When a young mother
tries to sell Grace a St Brigid cross made out of bulrush, meant to protect
from harm, fire and famine, the young woman notices a smell of mould and
realizes that these religious objects are indeterminately sold by everyone.
Further on in the novel, a priest approaches Grace and her companion on
the road to ask for help: he is looking for young people to transport a coffin
to the cemetery. The voice of her young deceased brother chimes in to put
Grace on guard against this potentially false priest: "Colly whispers, I'll bet

---

[10] *Ibid.*, 269.

[11] *Ibid.*, 188.

[12] The subject of religious salvation was informally discussed with the author during
his visit to Université Clermont Auvergne in October 2019. The choice of name of
the main character leads us to ponder on her salvation, both moral and physical.
Several incidents point to this: her near death experience at the end of the novel as
she communes with her deceased mother, her conversations with the ghost of the
victim of the holdup, whose first name is Mary and the final words of the novel,
"This life is light." 354

he's one of them fake priests wandering the roads, men dressed in cassocks asking for alms, taking their cassocks off at night and climbing into bed with widows and daughters, praising God and all the saints while trying to pierce their insides, and how can you know this man is telling the truth, that this isn't some scheme he's up to?"[13] Heralding a later episode where a lascivious pastor tries to bed Grace with impunity despite her severely malnourished state, the question of moral salvation appears to be at the very heart of the novel.

In contrast with the silence of the famine victims, language is often deceptive. The lush deep voice of a wandering priest resonates with that of an evangelistic pastor with a glib tongue announcing the end of creation as we know it and the imminent arrival of God's armies from the mountainous roads of the four corners of Ireland. This is the path of divine salvation, according to the evangelist whose gift of the gab drowns his public. For Grace, whose inability to speak persists because of the traumatic events linked to her journey, her name changes when she integrates the religious community. Henceforth she is known in the closed community as Mary Ezekial, the one who cannot speak. In chapter three of Ezekial, verse 26 we read: "I will make your tongue stick to the roof of your mouth so that you will be silent and unable to rebuke them, for they are a rebellious people."[14] Grace remains silent until the end of the novel. Under the authority of the sect, she undergoes a public confession in the form of a ceremony announced months in advance. Convinced of her disgrace, the wordplay is deliberate, the so-called purification is simply a pretext for the pastor to rape her, as he already has done with all the women who are systematically removed from the community if they fall pregnant. The pastor threatens Grace to emphasize her guilty state: "It is the devil who has gotten your tongue. It is the devil who will walk with you when I send you out on the road. You should think about that. Your soul in hell."[15]

Nevertheless, all words are silenced when the story of Grace's inner spiritual journey ends. She sits down on a rock from which, according to a legend recounted by her mother, the devil wrote the book of fate. The irony of the corrupted pastor's words permeates the final pages of the novel. The road becomes a type of palimpsest because her life, indeed her very survival, is intimately linked to the people she meets along the way and who write her

---

[13] *Ibid.*, 191.
[14] *The Bible*, New International Version, (Colorado: International Bible Society, 1983), 868
[15] *Grace, op.cit.*, 331.

story with her, in blood, mud, tears, or pure starvation. A totally secular vision of the sacred is represented in the final lines of the novel when Grace embraces the present moment as something beautiful and eternal. She finally discovers a physical and moral peace as the tortuous road gives way to a longed for safe destination. Paul Lynch allows us to delve further into the novel's ending, where we learn that Grace is pregnant, in the following extract:

> I seek always to give the fullest expression to our plight as human beings, to recognise that hell is a psychological place, and that heaven, or transcendence, is deliverance into acceptance and the fullest light of the self. Grace endures, but to do so she must first descend into the darkest places of the self, that becomes for her the atomisation of self. To emerge from a hell like that, and not be devoured by it, takes astonishing courage. My hope was that by the end of the book, that journey would take her to a place of spiritual grace, a position the religious would see as blessed, but that I would see as awakenment or enlightenment. She comes to understand that life is light, that it is fleeting, and also extraordinarily fragile. Hence the last line of the book. "This life is light."[16]

If Grace recounts "a story of the road,"[17] the story is often written despite the novel's namesake and outside of her will. She rarely finds herself in a position of force, having rather to adapt to negative circumstances. A beggar whom she meets on the road advises her to travel slowly and to be wary of other travellers who do not know where they are going. Grace learns that she is a blind traveller like all other human beings and that blindness is part of her very nature. Having become an orphan, as her father died long before and her mother succumbed to the famine, as did her brothers and sisters, Grace finds herself back in her hometown after years of travelling but nothing remains of her former life. The former partner of her mother does not recognize Grace when he offers her a ride in his gig. She realizes that she plays a random and haphazard role in society:

> She would like to say, you think you make your own choices in life but we are nothing but blind wanderers, moving from moment to moment, our blindness forever new to us. And to fully understand what this means is to accept something that is an outrage to most people. There are only the faces of where you are right now and when you try to look back the facts become a dream[18]

---

[16] Quoted from a personal email written by Paul Lynch of 9 December 2019.
[17] *Grace, op.cit.*, 123
[18] *Ibid.*, 344.

The sociopoetics of Grace's road reflect a specific time and place: the Ireland of the 1840s. She is both individual and all humanity on the road towards death, yet ironically towards life in a postapocalyptic time. The metaphysical road she takes leads to a place where she must become a member of society, an adult in the full sense of the term. As only the here and now counts and the rest is the stuff made of dreams, she can now become a true stakeholder in her destiny. She is no longer being controlled by events but has opened her eyes onto the new world she has found. Paul Lynch leaves us with a profoundly humanistic view of our innermost selves.

## Bibliography

Lynch, Paul. *Red Sky in Morning*. (London: Quercus, 2013)
—. *The Black Snow*. (London: Quercus, 2014)
—. *Grace*. London: (London: Oneworld, 2017) (translated into French by Marina Boraso, Paris: Albin Michel, 2019)
—. *Beyond the Sea*. (London: Oneworld, 2019)

# CHAPTER EIGHT

# TWO POEMS

# LYNETTE THORSTENSEN

### Road Trip -Take One

Eighteen years old we were,
       In one little car, a Renault,
four tall young women,
       Well, Marie-Jo wasn't tall
we drove from Paris to Portugal
       listening to our only cassette
but what a good one,
       Marianne Faithfull's
Broken English
       The freedom went to our heads
even though Adeline
       was the only one
who could actually drive
       We danced in night clubs
fended off ardent young men
       got shouted at for uncovering our breasts
on a beach on a Sunday
       in Spain, right next to a pretty little church
just as the congregation poured out
       We laughed and shrieked and drank
too much port in Oporto
       stayed too long in the surf
sat around a flickering fire of driftwood
       slept in damp sand under the stars
Driving back to France
       in a diagonal line from Madrid

Adeline fell asleep
        But I grabbed the wheel
and we lived to see another day
        many more jump-off-the-sand-dunes-joyous-days
how exquisite we were,
        we, wild things
Marie-Jo especially loved it all
        The three of us who remain are glad of this
Dear Marie-Jo died of cancer at the age of thirty-two.

# Road Trip – Take Two

Now in our sixties
my sister, in characteristic fashion
has seized the steering wheel
I'm in the passenger seat
which is where I like to be
musing over the beauty of a paper map and the arrival of
road signs

We have all of Australia in front of us
beware
too long in the middle and we could get bogged
run out of water
and fail, even in our thoughts,
to acknowledge country

We are equipped though,
a second-hand four-wheel drive, sat-nav phone, first-aid kit
Esky and ice, beer and white wine
First stop, beach camp
at Mystery Bay
Eurobodalla National Park

My sister floors it
she has always driven too fast
if always with skill
the gum trees speed by, so too the spectacular bays
Kingfisher blue, gold and foam

We bring our music to the road,
natural alchemy
for the opening credits of a movie with promise
our life of escapade
Ella, Billie, Janis, Amy, Marianne
come along for the ride

The car is parked now
next to the tent, safe under the Milky Way
my sister, at twilight
always a time fraught with risk

barely avoided a massive kangaroo
We gulp down our wine
hearts racing still, but
the road trip goes on.

# CHAPTER NINE

## *1 THE ROAD,* AN ARTIFICIAL INTELLIGENCE REVISITS THE ROAD TRIP ON THE TRACKS OF KEROUAC:[1] AN INTERVIEW

## DAVID DESRIMAIS

**Catherine Morgan-Proux: What is the founding story of *1 the Road*. What do we need to know about it?**

David Desrimais: There are several ways to tell that story but perhaps the easiest one is to get back to Ross Goodwin's initial idea. Ross is not a writer. He refers to himself as "not a poet". He is a technologist, yet he also has a background in writing as the ghost writer for Obama's first presidential campaign. He is used to using words as tools. At the same time, he is a very skilled technologist, especially in Artificial Intelligence. So, he combined these two passions - A.I. and literature - by constructing an artificial neural network and by feeding it with literature. The A.I. in *1 the Road* only had access to selected data that were books, novels, poetry selected by Ross, who "trained" the machine. At some point, he thought the machine was ready to write something, so he thought of using the car as a kind of pen. At the same time, he wanted to anchor this whole project in the American literary roots of the road trip and especially the route taken by Jack Kerouac in *On the Road,* so he put his machine in a car. On the outside of the car, he attached a video camera, a microphone, a clock and a G.P.S. connected to the machine. With this equipment the machine could "see" and "hear" the outside world for the first time. It had one thing to do and that was to write.

---

[1] In 2018, JBE Books (*Jean Boîte Editions)*, a publishing house in Paris published the experimental travel journal *1 the Road* "by" Ross Goodwin, the *writer of the writer.* The interview took place with Catherine Morgan-Proux on 20 July 2021.

The project was to follow one of the routes that Kerouac used in *On the Road*. He chose the third route that goes from Brooklyn to New Orleans and so off they went. For some reason the machine didn't start to write immediately which is interesting in itself because it prompts the question what triggered the machine to write? What is the inspiration? It is the eternal question: why do we write? Why do we say something when we could stay silent? These are all classic questions, but they are highlighted here by the fact this machine was given the ability to write. Indeed, after 30 minutes it wrote the first sentence of what was to become the book. And this opening sentence is an amazing one: "It was nine seventeen in the morning, and the house was heavy. It was seven minutes to ten o'clock in the morning, and it was the only good thing that had happened" which is a Nobel Prize start for a novel! It is beautiful. On the trip, sometimes the machine launched into writing. Sometimes it didn't and so on. At the end of the journey a huge manuscript of over 400 pages was produced.

As publishers, we did what publishers do: try to help recalibrate the manuscript and prepare it for the largest number of readers possible. Of course, there is no discussion possible with the machine. You can't question specific sentences, so we had to make choices about quantity. We worked with Ross to reduce the manuscript by removing blocks of text without changing any phrase or sentence. In the end, what motivated us was to have a book that you can actually read, from start to finish. Of course, in a similar way to Beat poetry, it takes you to a world of dreams and nightmares and uncommon ideas. Unlike a novel it has no plot. But I do take pleasure in reading it as it is in a format which I think is right. Above all, it embraces the idea of machine writing.

So, this is the creation story behind *1 the Road*. We call Ross Goodwin "*the writer of the writer.*" Our first idea was to attribute the book and the text to the machine itself which has a name, *Wordcar*. So, the initial project was *1 the Road by Wordcar* with the machine presented as the author. However, when we worked closely on this project with a research team from Google Arts and Culture labs in the United States, they came back with the interesting idea that if we were to present the machine as the author, we would fuel a debate. We were not sure that we wanted to lend such an approach to the book by suggesting that the author was being replaced. Not at all. It is about seeing the complexity of the ecosystem of who is writing. What is inspiration? What is going on there? So, we removed the machine from the cover to put the human back as *the writer of the writer*. In the end, we consider the machine as another tool for us (just as the pen is a tool) to get to this literary result. Ross used two tools: the machine and the car. As he explains in the introduction, the combination of those is really like using another tool, such as a typewriter. There is something between yourself and the text, whatever it is. Also, the machine says things that have emerged from a vast corpus of literature and poetry that was initially written by humans. So, I must say this machine is absolutely a tool that is used by humans. Rather than replacing creativity, we can consider it as a medium for creativity.

**CMP: This opens up different ways of thinking about authorship. It is very stimulating and illuminating, especially for those of us who are not from the world of technology and might find the concept of A.I. rather intimidating. What would Kerouac say about *1 the Road*?**

It is hard to imagine what he would say. It is not mimicking Kerouac or any of the Beat poets. It is really considering that they are part of a deep culture. I don't think Kerouac expected *On the Road* to become so important in literary and popular culture in the U.S. and around the world. What we have here takes inspiration from many well-known components of pop culture: reading literature, going on a road trip. All the references that have made this project possible are very familiar to everyone. The point is I don't know what Kerouac would have thought. At some point he might have thought this was way too close to what he did himself, he and his crew. But in our mind, it is also a way to appropriate and to re-appropriate this tradition. To consider and to look with new eyes at contemporary issues: our relationship with technology, the fact that sometimes we are slaves to a tool. It raises questions about how we re-appropriate these contemporary issues through a project that is rooted in literature and history.

I think the honest answer is that I don't actually care what Kerouac would have thought about this project because it is not really about him. *On the Road* has been digested by everyone and now it has become something else. *1 the Road* is a tool to address the issues of machines and their massive presence in our lives. A.I. is changing many things, from the price of a train ticket to the way we search for something online where our search choices can be predicted. A.I. is a critical issue for us to consider nowadays. This book is a way to appropriate it through the shared, reassuring medium that is literature. How do we flip A.I. in that way? In my opinion, that is one of the most interesting things, besides the fact that the machine was able to produce an unexpected text. It is very poetic in my view. Yes, this is strong poetry because it brings to light new ideas, new images and unexpected things. That's what good text and good art does.

**CMP: What about the roadscape in the text? Gas stations, car parks, motels…. In road narratives they usually punctuate the plot but here they are fully integrated into this road universe. What does *1 the Road* say about the idea of itinerary?**

DD: As the car is a pen and the car can only drive on roads, this whole book is about roadscapes. The whole context is the road. What does this machine have as a background to describe the roadscape? Ross told me that he specifically added books and essays about the Shoah to the corpus, including texts by Primo Levi as well as many other works. Bearing this in mind you will find, in parts, that there are often references to railroads with associated vocabulary such as barbed wire and fences. Ross wanted the machine to have a powerful corpus that included this literature. So, in terms of the roadscape, the machine has the possibility to focus on things based on material that is full of references to death and the Shoah. This is interesting because the roads they went through from Brooklyn to New Orleans have little to do with the Shoah and yet it is because of these tools that there are descriptions of what is happening on the side of the road.

This idea of the road as a whole, as an all-encompassing entity, is interesting. I don't think we have seen this before. Kerouac takes a journey on the road but at the end of the day he finds somewhere to eat, to sleep, and we are still with him when he is doing this. The text of *1 the Road* never leaves the road. There is no moment out of the road, there is no break, no going into a house. It is set exclusively on the road because the car can't go anywhere else. I have never thought about this before. This book exists only on the road. Exclusively on the road. No side moments. It is only the road.

**CMP: In *1 the Road*, there is <u>only</u> the road.**

DD: Exactly. That's interesting. I don't know if we can find many examples of this elsewhere.

**CMP: This book is unique in many ways, including that one! Thank you very much for your time.**

# CONTRIBUTORS

**Philippe Antoine** is Emeritus Professor of Nineteenth Century Literature at the Université Clermont Auvergne where he is a member of the research group *Centre de Recherches des Littératures et la Sociopoétique* (CELIS). His publications focus on non-fictional writing of the Romantic period, and especially Chateaubriand's works. He has participated in the publishing of the complete works and a dictionary dedicated to this author. He specializes in travel literature and was for many years in charge of the *Centre de Recherche sur la Littérature de Voyage* www.crlv.org, and editor of the online review *Viatica*. His published works include, *Quand le Voyage devient Promenade. Écritures du Voyage au temps du romantisme*, (Paris: Presses de l'Université Paris-Sorbonne, coll. "Imago Mundi," 2011) and *Les Récits de voyage de Chateaubriand. Contribution à l'étude d'un genre*, (Paris: Champion, 1997).

**Leisha Ashdown-Lecointre** has a PhD in Nineteenth Century French Literature and teaches at the Université Clermont Auvergne, where she is a member of the research institute, *Centre de Recherches des Littératures et la Sociopoétique (CELIS)*. Her research publications focus on the literary portrayal of the actor and pantomime in the nineteenth century. She has also published articles in other areas, including the theoretical links between Bourdieu and Maupassant's novels, correspondence between Flaubert and George Sand and the writings of the regional author Jean Aicard. She collaborated on an ANR project entitled *Therepsicore* led by the CELIS on provincial theatre during the French Revolution and First Empire. She has published several articles including, "Lettres et l'être du poète. La formation littéraire de Jean Aicard par sa correspondance" in *Le Chemin des correspondances et le champ poétique À la mémoire de Michael Pakenham.* (edited by Steve Murphy), (Paris: Classiques Garnier, coll. *Rencontres*, 159, 2016), 67-82 and "'Mon cher poëte, mon cher ami' : confrérie et amitié entre François Fabié et Gabriel Marc" in *François Fabié*, (edited by Michèle Gorenc and Jean-François Costes), (*Littérature en Lagast*, No. 10, June 2018), 19-37.

**Lambert Barthélémy** is a Lecturer in Comparative Literature at the Université de Montpellier III and is a member of the French Society of General and Comparative Literature. His many research publications are in the areas of the contemporary novel, and in particular on the relationship between literature and pictorial arts, fantasy aesthetics and environmental imagination, such as *Fictions contemporaines de l'errance: Peter Handke, Cormac McCarthy, Claude Simon.* Editions Classiques Garnier, 2012 ; "Langages de l'errance," in Cahiers de Marge, (Éditions Kimé, 2013), 165-175 and "(...) *le satori du transit (...)" ou : Les dromomanes du monde liquide (Rolin, Stasiuk, Vasset, Sinclair)*, in *Corps et Psyché*, 2021, 3. Specialized in German civilisation, literature and linguistics, he is a practising translator and is the founder of *Editions Grège* publishing house.

**Ted T. Cable** is Emeritus Professor at Kansas State University, USA and has served as a visiting professor in France He currently carries out heritage interpretation training worldwide, interpretive planning for parks and tourism venues, and does freelance writing for travel and nature magazines as well as script writing for interpretative audio trails. He is the author of 15 books specializing in Natural and Cultural Interpretation, Ecotourism, as well as Park and Natural Resource Management. His publications on interpreting from the road include *Driving Across Missouri. A Guide to I-70.* Lawrence, KS: University Press of Kansas, 2012 and *Driving across Kansas: A Guide to I-70: Newly Revised and Updated Edition.* Lawrence, KS: University Press of Kansas, 2017.

**David Desrimais** is the founder and director of JBE Books (*Jean Boîte Editions*) with Mathieu Cénac. He publishes books in the digital age, in the areas of art, humanities and poetry with publications distributed worldwide (in 15 countries). Within the Université Clermont Auvergne, David Desrimais has been working as an associate lecturer from 2016-2022) in a Master's of Publishing and is an associate researcher in the CELIS.

**Alain Montandon** is Emeritus Professor of General and Comparative Literature, at Université Clermont Auvergne, an honorary member of the *Institut Universitaire de France*, directs several literary collections and is also a member of the editorial committee of many reviews. He founded and directed the *Centre de Recherches sur les Littératures Modernes et Contemporaines* (CRLMC) until it became the *Centre de Recherches sur les Littératures et la Sociopoétique* (CELIS). He has authored over 20 books, 400 academic articles and has directed more than 70 collective volumes. He is currently in charge of the publication of the complete works of Théophile Gautier by Honoré Champion. Among his many publications are: *Sociopoétique de la promenade,* (Clermont-Ferrand: Presses Universitaires Blaise Pascal, 2000) and *Le Livre de l'hospitalité. Accueil de l'étranger dans l'histoire et les cultures* (edited by Alain Montandon), (Paris: Bayard, 2004).

**Catherine Morgan-Proux** is a lecturer at Université Clermont Auvergne where she is a member of the *Centre de Recherche sur les Littératures et la Sociopoétique.* (CELIS). After a PhD in American literature obtained from the University of La Réunion, she has focused on travel literature and has published mainly on travel texts by women. Her essays have appeared in *Genre et Dynamiques interculturelles : la transmission.* ed. Sophie Geoffroy. Paris: Harmattan, 2012 and "Women at the Wheel. The Sociopoetics of the Female Road Trip." *Sociopoétiques* online journal, Université Clermont Auvergne, December 2017. She was awarded a fellowship in 2019 at the Kluge Center in the Library of Congress in Washington D.C. to carry out a research project on cultural representations of women on the road.

**Isabel Oliveira** (formerly Martins) is Assistant Professor in NOVA FCSH (Faculty of Humanities and Social Sciences, New University of Lisbon, Portugal). She holds a PhD in Contemporary American literature: "The Good War: Perspectives and Contributions of the Second World War American Novel". Her main research and teaching interests are in four areas – Anglo-Portuguese Studies (mainly British and American travelers in Portugal), Portuguese-American Studies, North American Literature and Literary Translation. She has published and taught in these areas since 1983. Her latest publications are "Women's Diasporic Trajectories" in Katherine Vaz's *Our Lady of the Artichokes and Other Portuguese-American Stories* and a chapter in *American Studies Over Seas: (Multi)Vocal Exchanges Across the Atlantic* (vol. 2), edited by E. Medeiros da Silva, Margarida Vale de Gato, et al. Peter Lang Publishing, 2022.

**Melanie Schneider** studied Romance Studies, German Studies and Comparative Literary Studies in Frankfurt and Lyon. From 2021 to 2022 she held a research scholarship with the Institut franco-allemand de sciences historiques et sociales (IFRA-SHS)/ Institut francais Frankfurt. Since 2022, Melanie has been working as a research assistant at the Institute for Romance Studies at University Regensburg and she is also a research assistant at the Institute for Romance Studies at the Universität des Saarlandes. Her PhD project focuses on the cultural imagination of traffic jams in contemporary Francophone literature. Her research interests include 20th and 21st century French and German Literature, travel writing, road narratives and mobility studies.

**Lynette Thorstensen** is a New Zealander who has lived for twelve years in the Auvergne, France. Her poetry has been published in *Landfall* and *Takahē* magazines in New Zealand and *Southerly* magazine in Australia. Lynette Thorstensen's work also featured in *PN Review* in the United Kingdom. Her poetry has also featured in a range of media in the United Kingdom, the United States, New Zealand and Australia.